Paul
Gauguin's Son

© 2017, SAUGUS BOOKS
For this and other Saugus Books offerings go to:
https://www.facebook.com/Saugus-Books-508456039340536/
saugus.books@gmail.com

PAUL GAUGUIN'S SON: THE LIFE AND TIMES OF EMILE
GAUGUIN
ISBN-10: 0998588008 (soft cover)
ISBN-13: 9780998588001 (soft cover)

Disclaimer: In paraphrasing Emile Gauguin's letter and any other documents
provided, the authors have made every attempt to retain what they believe to
be the intended meaning, and the publisher regrets any references and remarks
that may appear to be prejudiced or biased that the present edition may contain. The authors have made every attempt at accuracy and apologize for any
statements deemed incorrect by others, including misspellings of names, places
or dates.

Special Note: A Kindle version will soon be available to aid readers to view and
hear links as well as search the text, and the photographs should be clearer.

Printed in the United States of America

Still, he remained a proud, engineer-adventurer-warrior leading rebel fighters cheating death in the northern Andes, constantly searching for work on three continents, continually facing financial collapse, fighting off hunger as a homeless transient in the American Great Depression.

Throughout this period his marriage, filled with passionate lovemaking and blistering anger, resulted in three beautiful children. But the relationship went through convulsive breakups, each followed by long periods of separation, and then, dizzying attempts at reconciliation ending abruptly each time in screamed pronouncements. Finally after the third try, Emile in blaze of fury said. "You are all dead to me!" and shunned four generations including his mother, brothers, wife, children and grandchildren for the rest of his life.

AND YET, SUDDENLY, AT life's darkest hour when he wrote his Colombian cousin, summarizing page-after-page his pathetic existence, almost as a miracle his life two-thirds over changed a year later to one of happiness and peace.

unhappy. Her name was Mette Gad. His father was also conflicted yet a happy, jaunty businessman, a Parisian and part-time artist, Paul Gauguin. Over time Mette would play a largely positive part in his upbringing. But Paul would spend increasingly less time as a father, yet still projected a powerful influence on Emile. Fatherhood responsibility was compromised by his preoccupation with his career, his uncontrollable obsession to paint. Although Paul came from a life of opulence, he soon renounced wealth, almost sneeringly expecting family and friends to help financially while he played the role of 'starving artist'.

But this was not the case for three of his ascendants: his maternal great-great-grandmother (Therese), her daughter (Flora) and her granddaughter (Aline). Go to Figure 1, the Tristan-Gauguin genealogy, below. They spent a good part of their energy struggling to acquire wealth, a rightful inheritance that nearly disappeared. And ironically, one could make the argument that it was their efforts that helped propel Emile's father to artistic stardom.

Of course there is much more to Emile's ascendants than the lack of wealth, or better, the desire to have it. But it is a good entry point to embrace their otherwise, noble characters. The long story of the search for a rightful inheritance is a good one. And it began with Emile's wealthy great-great-grandmother, Therese. One day, while living the grand life in her French villa, instantly … she became a widow and pauper. Her husband Mariano died, the French government viewed him as an enemy alien, did not recognize the validity of her marriage, and commandeered the villa. As a homeless aristocrat, she would not accept her new, lowly position and was convinced a huge inheritance belonged to her.

3Aline Marie Chazal (1825-1867) & Guillaume Clovis Pierre Gauguin Juranville (1814-1849).

    4Marie Fernande Marcellina Gauguin Chazal (1847-1918) & Juan Nepomuceno Uribe Buenaventura (1849-1896)

        5Pedro (1879-1966)

        5Carmen (1879-?)

        5Maria Elena (1880-1947)

    4Eugene Henri Paul Gauguin (1848-1903) & Mette Sophie Gad (1850-1920)

        5Emile Gauguin (1874-1955) & Olga von Hedemann (1882-1967)

            6Aline Gauguin (1909-1997)

            6Borge Emile Gauguin (1911-1974)

            6Pedro Maria Gauguin (1913-1996)

        5Aline Gauguin (1877-1897)

        5Clovis Gauguin (1878-1900)

        5Jean Rene Gauguin (1881- 1961)

        5Paul Rollon Gauguin (1883-1961)

Figure 1 Notes: We started Emile's genealogy here with his great-great-grandparents on his father's side: Mariano and Therese Tristan and his great-great-Uncle Pio Tristan. Mariano and Pio Tristan were brothers and are important persons in the narrative. Mariano was in France at his death and Pio lived for most of his long life in Peru. We refer to them as generation 1. Emile's great-grandmother Flora Tristan is generation 2 and so forth ending with Emile's children who are generation

and unknowingly played a brief, yet pivotal role in the young Gauguin's future and in the history of art. He was Gustave Arosa. Suffice to say, Arosa was wildly wealthy, lived in splendor and attracted a large circle of influential friends, forming a luxurious nexus for business, art and culture. And in 1861 the tiny Gauguin family consisting of Paul Gauguin, his sister and mother would enter the grandiose Arosa sphere. For David Sweetman [**Paul Gauguin's biographer in his excellent book and major resource for this book** *Paul Gauguin: A Life,* **1995**] just how the Gauguin's joined the Arosa family was a mystery. How could this unknown threesome, insignificant, living at the lower end of the economic spectrum, without any distinguishing features other than spunk, suddenly become associated with one of the wealthiest men in the Second Empire, one of the leading and renowned art collectors in France? The differences between the two families were as pronounced as black and white. Our guess is that few others interested in Gauguin history would not have known the reason either. But through our research we will reveal, in Chapter 3, how this interesting and historically critical and seemingly impossible association took place. This was a real-life, Cinderella tale. One that a cynic might offer 'only could have happened in Hollywood'.

For the moment all we need to say is that Gustave helped support the young Gauguin's for the next six years up until 1867 when Paul's mother Aline died at age 42; and then, he and his family took over their complete welfare and education until at least around the time Paul married in 1873.

A year or so later Paul's sister Marie seeing her happy brother, married a Colombian gentleman named Juan Nepomuceno Uribe Buenaventura, a well-to-do businessman from Colombia who was in France to cash in on the French construction of some newfangled canal through the Panamanian Isthmus in Colombia. His plan was to provide medical help for the construction personnel, namely the antimalarial drug, quinine, the crystalline alkaloid extracted from the bark of cinchona tree harvested for Juan by Peruvian Indians.

Juan had traveled to France to invest in the canal project with the possible support of Colombian investors, or he may have been employed by the creator and lead developer himself, Ferdinand de Lesseps. Given these possibilities his quinine business was probably the keystone to his economic presence in the project. But whatever the sources of his finances and enthusiasm, the future of the enterprise turned out to be ephemeral.

A painting of him (see Photographs I) shows a very distinguished gentleman in a dark suit and what seems to be a white, dress shirt. The portraitist was Laurent, famous at the time, in the style of Edouard Manet. Also, in the Photographs I section, there is a portrait of a middle-aged Marie made by a different painter years later in Bogota. It was in this environment that art, literature, politics and business were discussed, and large sums of money were being made, or lost.

Marie, having lived in Peru for about six years **[By then she and Paul were culturally Peruvian.]** and now with the Arosa's, she and her brother were perfectly bilingual. Married, her full name became Fernande Marcelline Marie Chazal Gauguin de

addition to tutoring Paul in painting technique, also taught his daughter Marguerite. She later became a professional painter speaking well for his teaching ability. Arosa was well known for his art collection, but it is interesting nonetheless, that he became a painter, too. He must have learned technique from the artists' works he collected and perhaps carefully studying the paintings in his vast collection. He not only amassed art but enmeshed his life in it. Curiously, despite Gustave's generous, avuncular interest in Paul's own development, Paul nastily bickered with him. This is not surprising because Paul bickered with many people, but there was another reason that may become clearer. Marie knowing her brother, took Gustave's side. [**No good deed goes unpunished.**]

EMILE IS SENT TO COPENHAGEN

The Spanish connection became more and more intense to Mette as she learned her husband was becoming (at least for her) too deeply involved with their revolutionary ideas. Considerable time and discussion was spent on politics in Spain, making Mette uneasy. Coming from a background of stable governments and 'reasonable' citizens she disapproved of such volatile, unreliable people. It is also possible that because her Spanish may not have been good enough, she felt secrets were being kept from her. Although Paul's financial situation in business improved, pleasing Mette, it was just a matter of time before he would become a full-time artist. So, Mette's outlook rose and fell with his shifting career tracks.

Paris. Indeed, you will read later that having his nationality switched at age six became a sore point, one that he would never give up. He always considered himself a Frenchman. And those early years had been imprinted in his being. Staying in Denmark for 20 some years would never be enough to make him a Dane.

While he was getting thorough schooling in Denmark, Mette and Paul's marriage was going from fabulous to bad in France, showing signs of total disintegration. True, despite the absence of Emile, the Uribe, Arosa and Gauguin families must have enjoyed each other's' company. For at least five years, and as their families grew and matured, get-togethers must have had as many as seven cousins that played together: Pedro, Carmen, Maria Elena, Aline, Clovis, Jean Rene, and Paul Rollon. One can imagine great family parties where the other Gauguin kids played with their Uribe cousins who were close to the same age. Of course Mette and Paul and Juan and Marie must have enjoyed the family get-togethers, too. But tragedy struck, for the first of several times. Suddenly and unexpectedly, little Carmen died. Despite the gloom of this sad loss, the families soldiered on. It is likely that even later the two families corresponded first as neighbors and then, later by letter, at a greater distance.

Emile's dad had a career change

But Paul Gauguin's career trajectory was changing: first, he thought seriously of becoming a full-time artist and, then, because of the new painting style, decided to go broke chasing

mind already a horrid Dane. At least Clovis, he felt, would get a 'proper' Parisian education, he could be more successful in molding him (he was too late with Emile) and mainly he could return to the heady, intellectual Parisian atmosphere where he could continue his main love: painting. But as far as Emile may have felt, he was dumped on again: this time he lost his father and his younger brother.

This bold plan of Paul's lacked some degree of foresight. His financial life continued to unravel and his family responsibility became frenzied. With Gustave dead his main financial backup was gone. He assumed that Marie's pity for him and little Clovis would be enough for her to approach Juan for support. But Marie was still angry over Paul's ungracious treatment of his benefactor, Gustave (Paul was sure that Gustave had his mother as a courtesan). So, working on her guilt, he finally succeeded briefly in getting Marie to take Clovis in for a while, but in a short time she returned him to Paul. Marie was just not sympathetic with her undisciplined brother; *why should she be responsible for his spawn* she may have asked herself. Mette, too, intent on revenging her husband, didn't seem to care much, either. Poor Clovis' life, it can be assumed, was not a happy one with a disinterested mother and aunt and a frazzled father. Paul's continued appeals to his sister and his wife, the mother of Clovis, went unheeded. According to Sweetman, Paul wanted desperately to go to Brittany but taking Clovis was problematic. Eventually Marie stepped in reluctantly to pay Clovis' school fees. Apparently this gesture was enough to allow Clovis to stay in Paris; but Marie, though she loved her

attempts to recover his investment loss were becoming futile. Juan's great-great-grandson Juan Nicolas Uribe has told us that because the Chinese were providing the canal company with extracts of the herb *Artemisia anua* which the Chinese claimed were more effective to fight malaria [**Artemisinin, the name of the purified medicine, the efficacy of which is still contested by the Center for Disease Control and Prevention in the US. wikipedia.org/wiki/Artemisia_annua**]

The Chinese were producing it at a lower unit cost than quinine, and convinced the canal company it was more effective. As the price of quinine fell, so did the Uribe family's fortune. However, yellow fever and malaria were taking their toll daily back in Colombia (the Isthmus of Panama still was Colombian territory) and the debacle of the French construction, further aided the demise of the project and the Uribe net worth.

To Paul, Marie appeared relatively wealthy, but this time her unwillingness to support his art career was based on real numbers. The Uribe's saw the writing on the wall. They planned to rescue their investment as much as possible and return to his home in Colombia. And in addition to Juan and Marie's financial health decline, Juan's physical health was in decline, too. It is likely that he contracted a tropical disease perhaps yellow fever. Together with the emotional toll: the dwindling of his monetary assets, and the actual infections themselves he fared no better than over half of the workers there. Eventually his luck ran out. Three years after he joined Marie and the kids in Bogota he died in his wife's arms in 1896 at the age of 47.

rytterskolers (rider schools) were established http://www.thor-shoj.dk/Rytterskoler_Dronningborg.HTM. Latin and Greek were required mainly for theology preparation. A small percent, those who could afford it, attended these private schools. Gymnasiums (high schools) though public, had tuition. Clearly Emile could speak French and Danish, and it is possible that Emile had more language training in school, and having associations with the Arosa and the Uribe families, must have spoken Spanish as well. It is no surprise that later he bragged he was good at languages.

In addition Mette's family made certain Emile's training was moved up a notch by sending him to the famed Soro Academy, a rytterskoler. And upper class it was. It is Denmark's oldest and most celebrated school dating back to 1140 AD. Officially founded in 1623 as Soro Academy by Christian IV it meant to train boys to become military officers and government leaders with preparatory courses for science, engineering and medicine. In Germany similar schools were called knight schools where we can imagine students were trained to lead men and fight on horseback, i.e. become knights. Attempts were made at the Soro Academy to have equal numbers of children from the aristocracy and from commoners. We have been led to believe that Emile came from the latter group. Located in rural surroundings near the small town of Soro it was about 50 miles from Copenhagen. Currently approximately 450 students attend, many locally and others as boarders from a distance. In short, Emile groomed to be among the elite Danes, had a super education which might explain his confidence, aloofness and ability

1921 in his Preface to a collection of his father's diaries claimed his mother was a saint.

EMILE GOES TO ENGINEERING SCHOOL

By 1891, Emile had become a very tall and handsome 17-year-old about to enter Den Polytekniske Laereanstalt (now Technical University of Denmark) for university training in structural and mechanical engineering. There, Emile attended classes to pass exams to become an engineer. We know he passed the first part of the exam for building and mechanical engineering in June/July 1897, the record persists to this day. He had to continue taking courses and take an exam to get the actual degree. But what happened next is a puzzle. It is possible he continued to take courses and the exam. There was a hint from some of the correspondence he was involved in a cheating incident which would have meant expulsion. But Ms. Annette Buhl now in charge of the academic records told us from the time he started in 1897 up to 1904 there is no record of any expulsion. If he did take the exam, he may have flunked. She went on to report that over the next couple of years only about 80% of the students passed. Perhaps, grandson Jacques had the best answer.

Jacques Gauguin M.D. wrote regarding his grandfather in an email dated May 15, 2008: "The story went like this...he was a member of the High Gentlemen's Club (one had to be two meters high) in Copenhagen where

DEATH COMES TO DENMARK

If a case could be made that Emile's youth was unhappy, it became even worse in 1897. His only sister, the vivacious 19-year-old Aline, died of pneumonia.

Aline was the apple of her father's eye, even though he had not seen her much for a decade; on the morning of January first, after a New Year's ball, she caught a cold, her family explained, on a rainy carriage ride home. But sadly the doctors could not control her fever and she died two days later. A simple head cold that was not attended to became a lethal case of pneumonia. She was 20. And the family needless to say was devastated.

A cynical view of the family situation would be that the social-climbing mother eager to have her daughter attend fancy parties to marry wealth and position abetted her willful daughter in her attempt to become popular with young scions, but with less than casual interest in her overall health. It might be this reasoning that Paul Gauguin used to blame his wife for Aline's death perhaps because he had to futilely strike out at his wife. Perhaps he felt that his wife did not raise Aline correctly, and because of that she would not have become an irresponsible teenager. Had Mette done a better job he reasoned, she would have been more careful during her illness. Although Paul did not see his daughter for six years, he so missed her growing up to become a beautiful young lady. [**Yet in his many letters to his friend Georges-Daniel de Monfreid, Paul mentions his family only twice: Aline's death and Emile's great height.**]

EMILE'S AND HIS SURVIVING BROTHERS' FUTURES

Emile's other brothers, Jean Rene and Paul Rollon who liked to call himself Pola, stayed in Demark and prospered. Pola became an architect and also painted and wrote, and Jean went on to become a celebrated sculptor getting his picture in the Danish Encyclopedia.

The next phase of Emile's future was in Colombia to be covered in the next section. But before we go there, it is intriguing to wonder why did he leave Denmark? Is it possible that Paul Gauguin's oldest son had inherited his father's wild longings for adventure? This positive reason might be partially true, but he may also have left because he was disappointed with his family, what was left of it, disgusted by the Danish norms, and humiliated by his failure to finish his degree. Had he simply wanted to escape? He had a life to lead and the deaths of his siblings told him to get busy living it.

One point we learned in our investigation was that Emile steadfastly thought of himself as French. We found numerous instances of his low impression of his 'assigned' country which likely came from the sum of negative impressions he experienced living there for 20 years. Now he saw himself as fully trained and ready for action, but somewhere else. Why not go visit his Aunt Marie in Colombia? It is likely she had extended an open invitation to her Danish nephews and sister-in-law? And Emile did have a cousin there who was studying to become an engineer. Sounded like a good idea.

CHAPTER 2

Emile's Incredible Great-Grandmother

THROUGHOUT THIS PROJECT WE WERE made aware of Emile's relationships, mainly with his almost worshipful feelings toward his father, but also his more or less perfunctory attitude toward his mother, brothers, and wife; and to a lesser extent, his three children. But our research did not yield evidence of his interest in his ascendants, particularly two critical ones: his paternal great-grandmother, Flora, and her daughter and his grandmother, Aline.

Who were these remarkable women? This chapter and the next will describe these important people that in their own right were responsible in producing Emile.

If he had known what our findings have told us, he would have been immensely proud. Both were heroic, dedicated and focused. His great-grandmother was a true rebel, a fighter for justice, a fearless, articulate writer and a courageous campaigner for human rights right up to her untimely death.

wealthy family had fled earlier along with thousands of others across the Pyrenees to Spain as a refugee of the Reign of Terror of Paris (1793-4). https://www.marxists.org/history/france/revolution/timeline.htm

According to Sweetman they married and shortly they moved back to France to a grandiose estate on the outskirts of Paris where Flora was born in 1803. Mariano was less dedicated to the Spanish throne than his brother Pio de Tristan and entertained at his villa many well-known people including Simon Bolivar who favored an independent South America. His brother Pio de Tristan, a fierce Spanish royalist, who had already led troops against the revolutionary army in France was opposed to Mariano's political beliefs left, likely in a huff, returning to Peru to manage the Tristan 'empire' that funded Mariano's lavish lifestyle in France.

Napoleon became emperor a year after Flora was born initiating the beginning of the end of Mariano's wealth. Napoleon confiscated all properties owned by foreigners. Suddenly Mariano died. Therese was a French citizen but she could not prove she was married to Mariano, and the huge estate became the property of the State of France. In quick order widow Therese, Flora and her young brother (who shortly died) became paupers and had to move to a hovel in Paris. Flora was six.

For years Therese with her own 'royal' roots dreamed that she would have her financial security restored to its original splendor. She supposedly paid no attention to the ambient squalor, perhaps suffering from a psychosis Sweetman noted in the letters she wrote to Pio de Tristan. As the years passed Therese

For the next five years while Therese reared Aline, Flora tried to find herself. Without little formal training (we know now she was an excellent writer) she was unable to get a 'good' job, she began working as a shop assistant nearby, then later as a governess in England. She had boundless energy but unformed ambitions. She had a brief affair with a ship captain in Paris which became the turning point of her career. Having recently returned from Peru he told her that she had a famous and powerful family there. Inside her a flash bulb went off. Recollections of her mother's rantings began to materialize. Perhaps she could stop working at dead-end jobs and become a collector, a collector of money. Her mother was right, she deserved a fortune.

She wrote her Uncle Pio a letter. Unlike her mother's letters, this one had authority. In its simplicity it had pizazz. This time he answered. Different from the many from her mother it demanded his attention. Something about this letter was important. She might have skills and talent after all. His answer explained that none of her father's money remained but he was enclosing a sizable check, 2,500 French Francs, drawn from his bank in Bordeaux. He never sent more. When the amount was almost gone, she put Aline in a boarding school and took off for Peru. She was 30.

FLORA'S SUCCESSFUL PERUVIAN ADVENTURE

After a three-and-one-half months voyage, according to Sweetman, she arrived only to find her uncle had 'escaped'. It seemed that he needed to plan how to deal with this plucky

no wife. His kids had been kidnapped. He searched for them for months to no avail. His printing business was in disarray. He was living almost like a homeless person. His name as an artist all but disappeared, the honors mistakenly went to his less talented older brother because he signed his name with the same initials. And this uppity, miserable excuse for a woman was the cause of it all. He needed revenge.

First he wanted his kids back. She had abducted them from him. Now he would abduct them from her. And he did. Goal one was achieved. But Flora fought back and retrieved them with the help of the police. Then, he re-abducted them and this time he compounded his crime: he tried to rape his daughter, Aline. He was imprisoned but the trial judge awarded him the child and his freedom because Flora could not prove anything. But his triumph was brief: Aline escaped.

Next, Chazal was so enraged he decided to take the law into his own hands. He would kill her, he would squash this insolent bug, and his revenge would be complete. Everything went well, he got a pistol and ammunition; he studied her daily routine; and one evening, he waited for her in the shadows when she was walking home. She came into sight, he drew his weapon, stepped out of the gloom and fired. When the smoke cleared, his estranged wife lay on the ground. Finally, he felt justice was served. *That bitch was dead. God had mercy.* Flora was 35.

But she did not die. The bullet missed vital organs. She recovered from the wound and in the trial according to Sweetman, the records noted she looked "wan and ethereally innocent" while he looked like a "mad animal". In the end, he was wrongly considered an anarchist and the founder of a weird religion (she knew, and was thereby guilty by association, the apostate cleric, Abbe Alphonse-Louis Constant, a proponent and reviver of Rosicrucianism). Was this a case of the pot lecturing the kettle? Some simply wrote her off as Paul Gauguin's grandmother. It is likely she may have had this patina, when family members described her to Emile: his dotty, great-granny Flora.

Even Sweetman wondered if her marriage was impacted by her rebellious attitude toward her husband implying it was her fault. And he pointed out her interest in a new religion that was gaining interest at the time, one with a female deity. However, the implication that she was involved in this religion does not gibe with the quote from her final book that we included below at chapter end. There, in an erudite manner she castigates the modern church for not following the Jesus model. We prefer to think the latter with her own, almost final words.

Despite her difficult marriage, she did have eventually a meaningful relationship with painter Jules Laure. His portrait of her she adored. Faithful and supportive he was her lover and soulmate in her final years, one who gave her sustenance in the face of public controversy, "police harassment and exhausting travel".

FLORA CONTINUES TO HAVE DETRACTORS

Even 170 or so years after her rediscovery as a force of social justice, the diatribes against her personality and lifestyle also continue to resurface. An article about Paul Gauguin recently written in Colombia by writer and poet Juan Manuel Roca

TABLE I. FLORA'S AND SIMON'S TIME LINES

Flora Tristan*	Simon Bolivar**
1803 born April 7 in Paris; her father (Mariano Tristan) and mother (Therese Laisnay). Flora may recall meeting Bolivar when he visited the family estate 1809 her father died, Flora and her mother became paupers 1819 worked as a colorist for Andre Chazal 1821 married Andre; had two sons 1825 Flora conceived in January; Flora left Andre; moved back to her mother's place; Aline was born in October 1825-32 Over the next years Flora worked at various jobs; learned of her rich relative in Peru 1833 wrote her Uncle Pio saying she knew Bolivar when she was a child; went to Peru 1834 returned to France; had troubles with Andre the next several years; continued her career - travels, research and writing 1838 *Peregrinations published, Andre attempted her murder and was imprisoned* *1838-44 worked ferociously on her research travels and writing*	1783 born in Caracas, Venezuela 1799 orphaned, educated in Spain 1802 finished education, married Maria Teresa in Madrid (she died 8 mons later in Venezuela), returned to France 1803 initiated as Freemason in Spain, visited Flora's father and mother over a few years 1804 lived in Napoleonic France, had more education; in Rome vowed to liberate colonies 1806 became Master Mason in Paris, visited Masonic lodges in London 1807 returned to Venezuela via US 1819 President of Gran Colombia for 11 years 1820-1 Freemasonry became legal again in South America; Masonic Lodge built in Lima 1824 assumed command of rebel forces in Peru; Elected President of Peru; awarded Freemason 33rd Inspector General 1825 President of the new country to be Bolivia for 5 months until January 1825; Dictator of Peru for six months

THE PROFESSIONAL FLORA

In any case, Flora's heroic, energetic and driven life had a purpose, one that was not to be denied. Her overarching goal was to assure worker's rights, human dignity and the deplorable plight of women and children. Her methods were to travel, interview people, take notes and publish them in books. But as a single woman then, making a living over her stipend from her uncle was a continual challenge. It began at age 30 on her Peruvian trip and continued up until her death. Her message today 170 some years later is still cogent, many of her demands are still not being met, and she has become the darling of human rights organizations throughout the World. Whether she made money from her books and how much is little known. But she is remembered in France. Her tomb in Paris still has thousands of visitors and is adorned with flowers daily.

Although Flora's creations did not fetch millions of dollars after her death, Paul Gauguin's grandmother's contributions to humanity became greater in the eyes of some than any canvas could ever do. The excerpt of her writing we quote below is a good example of her thinking, and one can only marvel at the incisiveness of her mind and ability to relay a basic human truth despite the consequences.

Being called a feminist depending on the company could be praise or an epithet. She called herself "a pariah", either as an apology to the then, male-dominated environment or to attract attention to her first book, *Peregrinations of a Pariah* (for a complete list of her works go to the dedicated section in the Appendix). In truth, she was a pioneer for human rights and

Monseigneur had seen the book and was not willing to receive it, --I took a card and wrote on it that I absolutely had to speak to the Bishop of Nimes about this book and that I would return the next day for the fourth time. –The concierge seemed to me very fearful of displeasing Monseigneur if my book was not returned to me. But I pressured this man, and he kept it.

"I arrived at eleven o'clock. –I was horribly ill, half-dead from fatigue. –My eyes were hollow, my complexion ghastly—and my expression bore traces of acute suffering. –The bishop's palace in Nimes is like all the palaces of these Monseigneurs – a large, beautiful courtyard, all covered with vines – a vestibule – at right a magnificent staircase leading to the apartments on the second floor—then an antechamber, a dining room, a large drawing room, a second one—a bedroom, and at the end a library-study—all looking out on a superb garden.—It was in this room that Monseigneur received me.

"For the first time I found a priest there.—I soon learned what his function was—he served as the "Bertrand" to Monseigneur. [**According to her biographer, Jules Peuch, she was referring to the unsavory and comedic characters, Robert Macaire and Bertrand, in the play L'Auberge des Andrets.**] It seems that in Nimes the need for a "Bertrand" makes itself felt.—In all the other episcopal palaces I have always found the Robert M[acaires] alone. Let us say

white, very beautiful teeth and white, well-cared-for hands—a black costume (cassock), but new, well cut and worn with an ease, and a graceful, bold bearing that perhaps was preferable to elegance.

"Ah! I must have made a singular contrast beside these two men.—I, in the opinion of the Holy Church, representing Satan—I was beautiful with that celestial beauty given by faith and love—my emaciated features and my expression of suffering revealed the fatigues of my mission—but my look, my voice, my firm, calm bearing revealed also the awareness that I had of my superiority over these two priests, who, in my opinion, represented the anti-Christ speaking in Christ's church, in Christ's name!—And in the name of this same Christ whom they were crucifying again in my person. Oh, those two "Satans" and I together in the study of the bishop certainly made a picture worthy of a great master!

"The bishop was seated in a large armchair express-ly made for him—but his pose had something forced and awkward about it.—The man in the cassock, seat-ed on a tapestried chair at the back of the study and in the corner of the casement window, was swinging his crossed legs in a very cavalier way.—I myself was four paces from the bishop on a superb damask armchair.—I entered and a glance at these two men was enough for me to know immediately with whom I was dealing.—I was in the presence of a bishop, a very mediocre man, and of a Jesuit of superior quality.

"Here, they began a long discussion carried on mainly by the Jesuit.—They subjected me to interrogations more malignantly Jesuitical than I had ever before encountered—and their manner, particularly that of the Jesuit, was so insolent, so unseemly and brutal, that it was indecent.

"I steadily countered their hostility with a coldness and a severity of conduct and a glacial scorn that ended by restraining the formidable Jesuit and much intimidating the bishop, who appeared to lack the strength to endure contests of this kind with a socialist.—I had begun by replying to the bishop that I was not a Catholic—he had asked me if I was at least a Christian in the sense that I believed in the divinity of Jesus Christ. Believe in the divinity, no—but believe in the excellence of certain principles preached by that superior genius, yes. He started a brutal discussion in which the two men wanted to make me confess that Christ was an imposter since He had said that He was the Son of God.—I told them that I excused Him for having spoken thus, but that he had been forced into it by the necessities of that time.—*"Then you excuse the lie?"*—*"Sometimes it can be useful."*—Another discussion here, and one in which the Jesuit treated Christ horribly, if one were to suppose Him not to be God.—Revolted by the cynical language of that man, in a moment of indignation I said to him:--*"Ah, monsieur, you slander Jesus your Master [illegible]!"*—My impulse had been

through Jesus Christ and in Jesus Christ that we are brothers, that we have love—otherwise, nothing.—*"So,"* I said to them, *"you do not believe that love is a law of God, innate in man—that this law of love is in his soul what the law of nourishment is in his flesh? And that in virtue of this law he loves and lives in the love of humanity?"*—And the two priests dared to answer: *"No—the law of love is not a law of God and innate in man—it is a law created by the spirit of Christ and the Catholic dogma."*—at these words I got up, threw a look of scornful pity at those two men and said to them:--*"Sirs, I will have to make a note of this conversation; it is remarkable. It is the first time that I have heard in a bishop's palace a priest slander Jesus and seen a bishop deny the power of God.—it is only in Nimes that one hears things like that..."*

"I left that palace beside myself with indignation and pity."

[As a note to you, the reader, do you think you could reason the way she did, under pressure of a hostile group? What is your position on the theology discussed? Could you support either side, if asked? You have one minute. Also, the foregoing clearly does not support a contention by others that Flora followed daffy religions.]

AT THIS POINT FLORA was mortally ill with typhoid fever. She died weeks later. Her daughter, Aline, living in Paris, was 19.

In someone so invisible, we were still able to find enough information to create a portrait. Much of what came out of our search was unpleasant, scary and depressing, not because of her, but a long list of misfortunes she faced and trespasses against her. Her story is one of heroic endurance in a sea of suffering, deprivation, sprinkled with a few joys and occasional salvations. She never had the opportunity to brag about her World-famous son. She never saw the birth of her grandchildren or their beginnings. Indeed, she never lived to see her daughter and son marry. She played her critcal role, played it well, and exited. Period. **[Information pertaining to Emile's forebears was paraphrased from Sweetman's excellent biography and from letters kindly provided by the Uribe family in Colombia.]**

ALINE'S SUFFERING STARTED EARLY

The list of her tribulations is long. When her mother Flora was pregnant with Aline, because her marriage was so bad, she left her husband, and Aline grew up without her father. Although Aline did not know it, she lived in poverty with her maternal grandmother while Flora worked at odd jobs. When Aline was about eight years old, Flora left for 15 months to visit Peru. Aline spent that time in a boarding school, likely a free school. Shortly after Flora returned, Aline was abducted by a stranger who she realized was her father. She was kept against her will, and suffered malnutrition. She was 10.

When she was 12, during this abusive confinement, she was sexually molested by her father; at 13 her father attempted

line, but I am sure she prayed a lot and Providence, if you will, intervened to help her at least five, key times without which perhaps fabulously valuable and beautiful paintings may never have been painted, large Colombian and European dynasties of Gauguin genes might never have been created, co-author Frank's cousin-in-law, Emile, may never have been born, and this book certainly never written.

Of all the people in the Gauguin line we researched, the least known yet the most mishap prone, the one needing the most inner strength, requiring the most familial, community and heavenly help not through any faults of her own, was the grandmother to Emile. Unfortunate circumstances happen to everyone, but with Aline they happened almost continually, perhaps sidelining, embittering, and life-changing many of us. But her story in addition to her own pluckiness involved key people, guardian angels if you will who appeared and intervened at critical points to aid her, to save the day, to help keep Aline Gauguin's destiny alive. But we have to conclude that it was Aline's inner strength, faith and immovable character that played the key roles in her day-to-day life.

Aline began life most likely in misery right out of *Les Miserables*. Before she arrived in life, her mother decided that her marital chaos had to end. Pregnant again she left Andre Chazal and moved in with her mother who likely was taking care of her two sons. For Flora, this was a return to the poverty she knew since her father died, which she escaped briefly to live and work with her husband. But now for Flora it meant freedom and peace to start over, working at odd jobs for low wages

awoke to find her father fondling her and touching her inappropriately. She fought him off, and he stopped before he could penetrate her.

The next morning Aline escaped and got word to her mother who had a man search the streets for her. Assuredly terrified her father would find her, she was continually on the move, hiding doorway-to-doorway, alley-to-alley. Once found she was returned to her mother who again had Andre arrested and jailed. This time the charges were more serious: attempted incest. But again the court released him because Flora could not prove it. Aline was 12.

Aline's next calamity happened at age 13. This time it only indirectly affected her. She was staying with her mom. Andre, her father, wanted revenge. He obtained a pistol, waited near Flora's apartment, and when she was returning home from work, he stepped out from the shadows and calmly discharged his weapon almost killing her mom. Again Andre was arrested, but now he went to jail, for many years.

Aline's source of terror had gone. She felt safer. No more kidnapping, no more assaults, no more freezing hovels, no more hunger. She returned to a higher level of poverty. True, she was spending her teen years without the nurture of a frequently absent mom, a 'permanently' jailed dad, and an addled grandmother. Missing out on support during her teenage years had to be considered minor compared to the continual fear. But the dread and nightmares must have persisted.

Her ordeal left us with many questions. Who was there to counsel her? Did she receive medical help? Did she receive

But then, when all seemed lost for Aline, out of nowhere a surrogate mother and protector appeared by her side. This was not just any person. She was the most famous woman in Europe: George Sand. [**According to her biographer, Benita Eisler, George Sand (aside from kings' mistresses, queens and princesses) decreed that novelist, George Sand, was the most famous woman in Europe.**] For Flora to have her as a close friend, and at her death, to have her act as surrogate mother, said a lot for the status of Ms. Tristan.

At an earlier time Sand and Flora knew each other campaigning together to reinstate divorce laws. But although Sands and Flora clashed continually, it is possible that she was there for Aline previously during Flora's many absences. Ms. Sand had earlier left her husband but still had a rich circle of friends and family. She already had two children of her own living with her in their late teens and early twenties and, then, was currently having an affair with Frederic Chopin. https://en.wikipedia.org/wiki/George_Sand

We can only guess that Flora had an extended collection of friends made up of artists, writers and intellectuals who likely also nurtured Aline. But one friend in particular, Flora instructed, that at her death, the wealthy author George Sand (nee Aurore-Lucile-Amandine Dupin) would care for Aline. At age 40 she stepped in masterfully serving as an adjunct parent, saw to her continued training at the highly rated Bascans school where she sent her own daughter. And in two years she

candidate, Louis-Napoleon Bonaparte. And when he won the election by a landslide, Clovis feared he might exact revenge and punishment against him as he did to his Uncle Zizi, deporting him. Better to deport himself. Aline's goal was simple, to support her family and to take on the task set by her mother and initiated by her grandmother years ago, to seek her rightful inheritance from the Tristan empire, namely from her Great Uncle Juan Pio de Tristan. Thus, with two small children in tow, Marie 2 and Paul 1, eager to leave, they booked passage on a small bark, the *Albert,* bound for Peru.

FROM TRAGEDY ON THE HIGH SEAS TO THE LAP OF LUXURY

As the sea breeze blew their stress away, they thought of the exciting new life that awaited them. Optimism bloomed afresh. However, things did not go well. Near the end of a three-month-long, treacherous voyage and after passing through the stormy Strait of Magellan, the ship anchored off the shore near Fort Bulnes to take on fresh water. Relieved, the passengers went ashore for a brief respite. In all the excitement and uncertainty of the process of climbing off a perfectly good ship and stepping onto a small, pitching whale boat, Clovis dropped dead of an aneurism. In an instant Aline's plans suffered a reversal without a Plan B. Widowed and with great sadness, Aline buried her dear love and her kids' father. We know that Clovis was buried there because of a recent DNA analysis of bones exhumed from the fort's graveyard (see

fantasy. And as the years passed by, the Tristan's loved their new cousins, as we learned from letters, more and more. But the protective screen of the Tristan world that she enjoyed was about to come apart. Uncle Pio Tristan realized that he, his family and his empire could be coming to a troubling end. His son-in-law Jose Rufino Pompeyo Eschenique could not wait for the promised Peruvian presidency, but perhaps feeling a double-cross, he decided to stage a *coup d'etat* against the current government. Pio, the seasoned politician and military strategist, realized it was premature, poorly planned and could well backfire. If it did, it could well cause serious complications, we think, to Aline and her kids, to get involved in a dangerous situation that could include confiscation of property, trials, and even executions. If that happened, Aline and her kids may not have financial support or a place to live, if indeed, they were allowed to live.

For this reason, Uncle Pio, may have felt the young Gauguin family should return to France and her father-in-law as soon as possible. But could they do the treacherous, three-and-one-half-months trip safely by themselves? The perfect solution may have presented itself: they could travel with Cousin Julio who we guess was sailing to France to work and study with a wealthy business friend of the family as well as to escape any retribution against the Royalists.

We are not sure how Julio was related to the Tristan or the Echenique families, but Julio was going to play a major role in protecting and perhaps guiding Aline, the holder of the

but where at least he became well versed in the Bible. Paul's behavior became more obstreperous and learning became more difficult.

According to Sweetman, when Aline saw that there was almost no chance of her getting little, if any, money from the Gauguin estate, she moved to Paris and opened a seamstress shop. Paul wrote later they were never in poverty but lived very simply, since she did get a regular stipend from Uncle Pio. In one of his letters in 1855 he told Aline about the money she is getting. He admitted it was not much by Tristan standards, but he asked her to assure Mr."L" his French banker, that *he is good for it.* [Mr. "L" was Pio's banker and although Uncle Pio refers to him twice, we could only make out the first letter of his name.] He reminded her the banker would send Aline checks quarterly which she was to cash. Also, she may have received a tiny compensation from her father-in-law's estate. Thus, she was independent at least for the next five years. Uncle Pio died in 1860 but it is possible that he put extra money into the French account beforehand. Our impression from the letters was that he was giving money to Aline against his family's wishes who were going to put an end to the stipend upon his death.

GUSTAVE AROSA: THE NEXT ANGEL

Sweetman told us that a new person entered the Gauguin orbit: Jean Dominique Gustave Arosa. He will turn out to be the final and ultimate savior of the fragile Gauguin threesome. The Arosa family wealth, starting with Gustave's father, Francois Ezechiel,

voyage from Peru to Paris (recall our above story that we speculated Pio may have wanted them to travel together for safety).
For the 1863 letter stated that Julio lived in Paris since 1855,
the time Aline arrived in Paris supporting our conclusion they
likely traveled together. **[How many Peruvian, France-bound
ships were there at that date?]** And we know absolutely from
this letter that Julio worked for Gustave Arosa, supporting
Sweetman's guess about a Peruvian connection. As mentioned
above Uncle Pio may have used his Parisian associates to give
Julio a position with a colleague, Gustave Arosa.

All Sweetman was able to find was that 1861 was the first
time the names Aline Gauguin and Gustave Arosa were mentioned together in the sources he reviewed. We know that Julio
was in Paris working for Gustave during Aline's five-year stay
in Orleans, and perhaps Julio wrote Aline that when it became
clear that Guillaume's bequest would be small, she should move
to Paris, likely telling her he had wealthy clients who would buy
her dresses.

Because Sweetman later claimed that Gustave funded what
he guessed was the poorly-paying seamstress shop of Aline's, he
supposed there might have been a quid pro quo, that is, she was
his plaything. Sweetman admits he has no proof, but cited indi-
rect examples to support his conjecture such as: (1.) He had other prior liaisons, (2.) he lived in and belonged to a milieu setting
low rank to morality, (3.) his married sister lived openly with
an unmarried painter, and (4.) his brother kept Clementine de
Bussy, also a seamstress, the aunt of the boy who would change
the spelling of his last name and become the famous, Claude

her, he honored her. And eventually he came to worship this saintly woman. Rarely does one meet such a personage. We are sure that he sought all sorts of medical help for Aline's increasing health problems. And he spared no expense for her children. They became his responsibility, his mission, his ministry. This time he could put his fortune to work on a beneficial crusade, instead of satisfying his whims.

Another aspect of Aline brought up earlier was that George Sand was her successor 'mother'. It is likely that Gustave knew of, if not actually acquainted with, the renowned writer, the first woman in Europe to become a best-selling author. This association, too, must have given Gustave awe. We would not be surprised the Mme. Arosa also supported his crusade.

He was unstinting in his support for Paul, seeing that he had proper schooling (to no avail), providing cultural nurturing in Gustave's world of art, teaching him painting techniques, and when he was older, feeling he had no future as a painter, paid for his schooling to become a naval officer [**Paul practically flunked out, but became skillful at fencing.**] After Paul's fighting in the short Franco-Prussian War, Gustave got him a job at Bertin, and introduced him to Mette Gad, his future wife, to list some of his contributions. Curiously, Paul had little respect for Gustave never appreciating his assistance. Sweetman used this behavior to support his guess that Paul may have suspected that Gustave was bedding his mother. But bad, unappreciative behavior was Paul's signature. Gustave was not the first or the last person Paul dissed. And Gustave paid little

with the beautiful penmanship skill, and ... patience. Whereas phone, text and email exchange takes seconds, a tweet or Facebook entry may take longer and a bit more for memes and photos. International air mail letters will take days. But in 1855 a letter exchange from Paris to Lima and back to Paris by ship would take over seven months.

Aline's daughter Marie saved a number of letters her mother received and thinking they might be valuable, brought them with her to Colombia. Her children and grandchildren also were cognizant of their value as did her great-great-grandson Juan Nicolas Uribe Uribe-Holguin who graciously shared them with us. One set came from Uncle Pio's granddaughter Mercedes. They were likely the same age and both became good friends during Aline's time in Peru. These would have likely have given us a picture of two pals communicating, a female perspective. Unfortunately they were so faded that they were unreadable, and our hopes to eavesdrop faded with them. [**Marie's letters were unavailable.**]

As mentioned above we were given some fairly legible letters Uncle Pio sent to Aline after she returned from Peru and one from a Peruvian cousin, Julio, some years later thanks to the careful archive-keeping of the Uribe-Gauguin descendants. And thanks to our team of transcribers and translators, we were able to reconstruct a tiny, intriguing bit of history from the two men.

Great Uncle Pio's letters were sent to Orleans around 1855 the one from Julio Fernandez to her in 1863 at her apartment/ shop at a somewhat fashionable address in Paris [**The same address that Sweetman published**]. These gems in Spanish and

also avoiding possible trials for insubordination; or worse, treason ending in imprisonment or executions. As it turned out the Constitutionalists were magnanimous, supporting the idea that forgiveness was a better strategy than revenge. The new government needed trained, dedicated people for Peru to become a successful, independent country on the World stage.]

The next letter is the important one. Written by Julio, perhaps a cousin, it implies a special relationship with Aline, and it tells us about his association with Gustave Arosa. Paraphrasing his November 11, 1863 letter in perfect French from Lima, Peru, he started with instead of "Dear Aline" he chose "Dear and Good Aline". He went on to write that he had read her letter written less than a month earlier October 22 to his mother complaining of Julio's failure to write her, unfairly accusing him of being forgetful and insensitive. He went on to say he could have written but he was entirely focused on catching up on his long absence from his home and family.

[Apparently he had already received a letter from Aline and he had put off answering her. Then, when she wrote to his mother accusing him that he was forgetful, he decided still not to write. When he finally did write, he angrily explained that his tardiness was because of his long absence, not his forgetfulness; that he had been too busy visiting with and enjoying his family and friends. Still, with all this squabbling, there might have been something between her and him, he did not want to deal with. Perhaps, this current letter from Aline was so angry and petulant that he

her impatience and frenzy. We will have to be content with our questions until more letters surface that are sufficiently legible.]

Julio went on to write that he arrived in Lima on July 23 experiencing a long and dangerous voyage: 108 days long (See Table II) with many storms remarking that he thought that his life was over in the icy waters of Cape Horn. He was so grateful to have survived and to be finally in his mother's loving arms. He noted that Aline could only imagine the great joy he felt seeing his mother again and the rest of the family after an eight year absence. He said it was only with the help of God that he survived. He said his mother was better and more loving than ever. [Do you buy all these arguments? Is Julio trying to wriggle out of something?]

He remarked that now he no longer felt the extreme pain and difficulties he had in Paris. Only rarely, now, he said do they enter his thoughts. If they do, it is only infrequently. He philosophized that the human psychology compensates for the horror he felt and that they are no more than a bad dream now. [His description of the horrors of the crossing was very interesting, but we suspect that he was using this experience to gain her sympathy and as a further excuse for not writing. There must have been a more valid reason he was not sharing with her but hints at it with his difficulties and pains he experienced in Paris, that only now he is beginning to forget. We are curious about what these experiences, but there are few clues. We can only imagine that he was severely injured or imprisoned. In another 1855 letter to Aline, Uncle

the home he returned to. **But although she asked to tell her
many things, he did not, at least in this letter. We under-
lined 'devilish' to gain the reader's attention to Paul's ongo-
ing, well-known, bad behavior.**]

He wrote to give his regards to the Arosa family and that
he thinks about them often, particularly his old boss, Gustave.
But he did not write him directly because he did not want to
burden them or force them to reply to him personally. [**Here it
is! Gustave Arosa was Julio's boss! And, as we implied, his
employment was the basis for the Gauguin-Arosa relationship. The letter did not indicate a close relationship with
the Arosa's because he asked Aline to make the salutations.
Perhaps this affectation of deference was typical of the day,
but it implied to us that the boss-employee relationship was
a wall of separation making him feel he was not at the same
level professionally or socially, or simply one of age. Could
it have been he was lazy? Or was there something more
embarrassing?**]

Julio continued to finish up the letter, telling Aline very little, but simply trying to make polite and trite phrasing, with a
little dig at the obstreperous Paul. Yet at the same time indicated
he had a more relaxed relationship with Gustave's jolly brother
Achilles referring to his kind attention to him when he departed.
He closed with affectionate reference to Marie and Paul, and to
Aline also telling her that he thinks of her with high esteem wishing her the best for her future life. [**Achilles was Gustave Arosa's
brother with whom Julio by the tone of this letter had a more
relaxed relationship and perhaps that Achilles was less formal**

TABLE II. OCEAN TRAVEL IN DISTANCE AND TIME

TRIP	MILES	DAYS (SAIL)	DAYS (STEAM)
Paris - Lima	12,362	111 [1,2]	35
Paris - New York	3,631	35	9.5 [3]
New York – Havana	1,300	13	4 [3]
Havana – Barranquilla	971	9	3
Paris – Panama	5,400	52	16
New York – Copenhagen	3,843	34	11

Ocean travel in the 19th Century was long, expensive and dangerous. Yet the brave people in this book who had the money did this at the drop of a hat. This table is meant to show the huge amounts of time the people in this book (or their letters) spent traveling by ship in the period from 1840 to 1905.

Travel times marked by superscripts were given by the travelers ([1]Flora, [2]Julio, and [3]Pedro Uribe) in their letters or travel documents. These times were used to calculate ship speed which then was used to calculate the times of the other voyages. Sailing ship speeds averaged were 112 miles a day (the average of Julio's 108-days trip and Flora's 113-days trip). Steamship speeds of the Paris-New York and the New York-Havana trips reported by Pedro Uribe (see Appendix) tripled the speed on average to about 354 miles a day. Distances were approximations based on data mainly from air flights, but also from letters and maps. Trip times varied considerably because of wind, currents, ship length and helmsman's skill, but also because of the

ALINE'S FINAL ACT

Aline's final tragedy occurred in 1867. After a long illness, Aline succumbed.

It was then that the angel of death made his appearance: at the age of 42 nearly the same age as her mother. This had to be traumatic for Marie 20 and Paul 18, but at least they had the support and comfort of the Arosa family.

CURIOUSLY A SIMILAR DARK period awaited her yet-to-be born grandson, Emile. But first we have to move forward to 1900 and the ship Emile is going to take to the New World.

sister, Auntie Marie, in Bogota. Her daughter Maria Elena was there, but her son Pedro was away at school in Switzerland. Emile must have known them from his Paris days. It was also likely that Emile already knew some Spanish. So, this was not a big adventure in the great scheme of things. His great-grandmother and grandmother had already traveled to South America. And like them, he planned a safe landing zone, indeed in the lap of luxury; but despite his careful planning, life-threatening adventure and prestige-threatening humiliation awaited him.

As we speculated in Chapter 1, we will never know the ultimate reason why Emile left Denmark, but there were strong driving forces and any one would have worked. First, it was an extremely sad time for the Gauguin family. It would be understandable if his mother, Mette, felt forsaken amid her devastating sadness to have buried two of her children in the last three years without the comfort, understanding and support of their father, Paul, who was to finish out the remaining three years of his life in French Polynesia. Mette, who lived her life in a strict, disciplined way, still must have felt insult to injury with her eldest son's departure without his having finished the requirements needed to graduate with an engineering degree. Without one he might never find employment in Denmark. And that might have been the answer. His Aunt Marie may have assured him he could obtain an engineering job very easily in Colombia.

This was Emile's first transoceanic trip, and it must have been exciting. The hubbub of getting off from his mother nagging if he had packed everything, to climbing aboard, to waving

his Aunt Marie Gauguin de Uribe some years earlier in the late 1800s. Bogota poet and writer Juan Manual Roca with muted humor retold a story he must have heard about her arrival, how she had to take a river steamer on the Magdalena River to the bustling town of Honda where mules loaded with all her material belongings from her swank Parisian apartment including tapestries, paintings, decorations and ornate furniture on the backs of mules.

The identical trip was made five years later after Emile arrived by his cousin, Pedro (Marie Gauguin de Uribe's son) who detailed in the Appendix his homeward bound trip after finishing university in Switzerland. Pedro in the thorough detail of a graduate engineer wrote that it was about 720 kilometers (450 miles) as the crow flies taking him 17 days from Puerto Colombia to Bogota. He arrived by ship at Puerto Colombia January 24, 1905, arrived by tram in Barranquilla later that morning, departed by river boat the next day. The boat arrived in La Dorada and in Honda after 12 days stopping each night to load and unload. Night travel was likely out because of navigation dangers. Then, they traveled by mule train the remaining 96 kilometers (60 miles), climbing nearly 12,800 meters (8,000 feet) over a mountain trail (which is now Route 50), stopping for the night at villages or hostelries such as Gainete, Vergel, and Chimbe, to feed, water, and rest the mules and travelers before arriving in Bogota. This was the trip that any visitor had to take an adventure in itself, and knowing this ordeal awaited their return, would likely decide to stay in Colombia for an extended visit.

impressions of the dazzlingly bright, strikingly new and color-ful landscape - and cityscape - filled with strange and clamor-ous sounds and smells and people of all shades of color, set off by a horizon lined with mountain peaks. Street vendors sell-ing unknown fruits of different colors, cut into bite-sized cubes ready to eat. Or there were snacks of freshly cooked meats and breads being sold at stands or carts. Newspapers and books and clothing and tools were being hawked in a riotous polyphony of voices and music. Beautiful, sensuous in any view, but amaz-ingly vibrant to a man who spent most of his life in a gray, cloudy, rainy atmosphere, a country that was flat and bland and austere.

Paying off the mule train drover, he transferred his bags to a horse-drawn taxi. He fumbled for the address. The cabby saw the fancy destination and began to take this dusty disrepu-table-looking, foreign monster a bit more seriously. Soon, clat-tering through numbers of streets and different neighborhoods he was there. The cab took him into the courtyard of a huge colonial townhouse, where Aunt Marie lived at the corner of 1900 Calle 13 and Carrera 13, a fashionable and very old part of town. The family nicknamed the house: 'Trece-trece' or 'Thirteen-thirteen.

Aunt Marie and the family had been expecting him for maybe a week or two. They found out when the next mule train was due. And the staccato sounds of the horse and cab in the cobbled courtyard was the alarm they were all expecting. Then, one of her nephews in the self-appointed role of sentinel screamed, *"Here comes Primo Emile!"*

pictures in Photographs II) and they had already some of ten children. So, this odd and massive relative who came by ship from a strange land would certainly become a center of attraction. Then, when more relatives and friends accumulated it became a mob. In addition there was Juan's maternal family, the Buenaventura's which also was likely large and who played an important role in the young Gauguin-Uribe family. One of Pedro's Buenaventura uncles paid for his entire education including getting his engineering degree. Thus, although the exact size is unknown, but we can be sure of one thing: Emile fell into a large, loving, extended family, a sea change from his grief-ridden, austere mother and remaining brothers.

To get an idea of the color and warmth of Emile's new environment, Google Candelaria-Bogota (or go to http://thecolombiatravelguide.com/photos/la-candelaria-bogota-5/)

Unfortunately, Marie's house (and her neighborhood) was replaced by a rather colorless, modern cluster of shops and medium-rise apartment buildings which can be viewed by Google Maps (at Calle 13, Carrera 13). You will see a store at ground level named El Gran Papeleria Trece (Big Thirteen Stationery store). However, we were led to believe that the original house was a grand, colonial building with a courtyard. And thanks to the internet we found a photo of such a place in nearby Candelaria. You can view a wonderful 360 degree shot taken by Jorge Wilsor Barco Arcila (go to https://www.google.com/maps/@4.5947289,-74.0761728,3a,75y,59h,90t/data=!3m7!1e1!3m5!1syuPyFK6dGRYAAAGu5vGqTA!2e0!3e11!7i3840!8i1920). By clicking on the compass needle, one can view the entire house and courtyard.

spoke of the beauty of the tropical surroundings and the native dancers. But we wondered 'why' he was on this trip? It is possible that after the war, he took this long trip with other men to get out of town to avoid retributions. Although he was on the losing side, perhaps the others in his group were too. Is it likely opponents may have been seeking revenge? It could be that Aunt Marie serving as his surrogate mother counseled him to leave until things calmed down, and she helped finance it. Perhaps Aunt Marie may have thought a trip of this sort would be therapeutic relieving him of the stress of war and the killing what we now call post-traumatic stress disorder (PTSD). A less dramatic reason was that it was simply an engineering project that involved travel.

The answer as to when and how Emile did finally hear about his dad's death, we have directly from him. In a 1938 letter to his Cousin Maria Elena he recalled how he learned of the death and intriguing information of his aunt's feelings about her brother. **[This 30-page letter was Emile's highly detailed autobiography of his time in Colombia and the US. We will refer to it often. More information about this important document lies in the section HOW THIS BOOK CAME TO BE WRITTEN, p.255.]**

Emile wrote that while visiting Don Paco Duque's news agency a family friend, Alfredo Venquechea handed him a copy of *Mercure de France* the famous and very old French literary magazine with an obituary of his father, Paul.

This may not have been very hot news for Bogota but it was to Emile. He paid for the magazine and ran home excitedly

friend in common she might remember, Don Epifanio, who remarked that the only really good painter was Velasquez, but there were others, of course, that could be included in his 'hall of fame' which Emile sardonically implied, could be a Gauguin or two. Epifanio went on exclaiming that he was sure that the Archbishop of Bogota was going to create a showroom in the Cathedral of Saint John in Engativa (a poor section of Bogota) for paintings of varied quality **[Epifanio was likely the portraitist, Epifanio Garay. See pp.375 and 382].**

Emile added that his father's fame by 1938 has reached such prominence to become a curse to him, whereby his own shortcomings will be more critically judged. He often denied any relationship when people asked. He sneered that the rest of his family in Denmark were less cautious. This 'curse' theme continues elsewhere in the letter and was also found in a letter of authorization to his father's old friend, Georges-Daniel de Monfreid.

[We must add here that at the same time Emile wrote to his cousin nostalgically of his great life in Colombia he was suffering in the midst of the Great Depression, desperate, poor, often hungry, currently unemployed as millions of others with little hope that the economy, his and that of the US, would soon, if ever, recover.]

But the trip Emile told about in the Florida newspaper must have lasted less than a year, probably several months, and Paul must have died near its end. Given the time it took for the information to get from Tahiti to Paris, the time to publish it and them to ship the magazine to Colombia, we calculate a minimum of 74 days (see Table II on travel times in Chapter 3).

and now for the first time, we can bring forth their material about Emile and related stuff about the Gauguin's. Basically the Uribe team provided enough bits and pieces to gain a skeletal background for 40 years of Emile's life or the missing half. One could almost say they were saving it for us.

Having said some of this elsewhere in the book, that the information provided by Team-Uribe answered a number of key questions and provided entirely new information about Emile and several generations before him. And although many questions are still unanswered, a credible story is now available. In assembling the data, distant cousins who only knew of each other have actually gotten together for the first time to help us in our project.

As a byproduct we now have a fairly complete family tree (see Appendix, Figure 2) thanks to Peruvian genealogist Francisco J. Carbone who died shortly after giving us a preliminary family tree. Subsequently the tree was appended, corrected, updated by Carmen Iriarte Uribe-Holguin, Juan Nicolas Uribe-Holguin Uribe and his 93-year-old mother Margot Uribe Gauguin Torres.

THE HISTORY OF THE EARLY COLOMBIAN URIBE-GAUGUIN'S

The branch of the current Uribe family of Bogota that carries the Gauguin genes started small with the three children of Juan Nepomuceno Uribe Buenaventura and Marie Chazal Gauguin de Uribe.

and in those times before modern medicine, death often came prematurely giving families then, a constant view of the continuum. Just as Mette, Emile's mother, suffered losses through numerous deaths in her family, Paul Gauguin's sister Marie also suffered. Her mother died prematurely in her 40's, then she lost her daughter Carmen at a young age in Paris, and her husband Juan Uribe who had died at the age of 47, and then she lost her granddaughter Consuelo at age nine.   But despite these losses Marie marched on with great fortitude and optimism. She still was blessed with her children Maria Elena and Pedro whose vigorous families we are now able to introduce.

MARIA ELENA

Maria Elena married Miguel Saturnino Uribe-Holguin and produced 10 children. Pedro married Elena Torres and had six more children. These offspring of Maria Elena and Pedro went on to create a large number of descendants, at last approximation, at least: 130, and about half of them are still living (see Figure 2 in the Appendix).

Emile knew both Maria Elena and Pedro in Paris as children and possibly later when they may have communicated through letters. When Emile arrived in Bogota, he got to know her more as a married, young adult. See Photographs II. Her husband Miguel Saturnino Uribe-Holguin brought the Uribe name into the family again. But both Uribe families are not related. Juan Nicolas said that the Uribe-Holguin family was from the northern State of Santander and was very wealthy.

PEDRO

One person who was not there when Emile joined the Uribe clan was his Cousin Pedro who was in Switzerland, studying engineering at the University of Lausanne. When Pedro did return in 1905 to Bogota, he probably visited briefly with his Cousin Emile. It is possible they may have remembered each other from their Paris days and perhaps Emile may have had a trip or two to Paris during his school vacations. Their association together might have involved work for a short time before Emile left for Sogamoso. However, it is curious that Pedro's name is only mentioned once in passing in Emile's 1938 letter. Nor did he ask after him. This leads us to believe that their relationship was not close. It is possible because Emile's training may have been shorter and less dignified than Pedro's, there was an educational and sociological chasm between the two.

We know from his curriculum vitae (see Appendix) that following his schooling Pedro began working for the local government. He became recognized by President General Reyes for building a controversial canal in Bogota to stop flooding of the San Agustin River. Then he moved to the national level (Department of Public Works). From 1910 to 1914 he was in charge of constructing railroad tunnels in the Buenaventura region in the west of the country, and after that, he moved back to the Department of Public Works until 1918. It is possible that he saw Emile during short visits to Bogota. But from what we could gather both men were devoted to their careers in separate locations.

Pedro was an exceptional student and later, a highly regarded engineer. He won many awards including Colombia's highest

in 2016 she was the family matriarch and repository of much family history. We were grateful to talk with her briefly getting genealogical questions answered, that gave us a better idea of the Uribe family Emile was likely to have known. She told us a story that Maria Elena tried unsuccessfully to match him up with a wealthy Colombian woman, but he eventually refused. She tried and tried, but Emile was adamant. He simply may not have wanted to marry at that time. Perhaps he did not want to displease his mother. Her wealth, as we became more aware later, may have been a factor. Emile, we concluded, rarely aspired to be rich. Indeed, with one exception a few years later, he shunned wealth, wanting only enough to live and be happy. This is the only 'Emile story' the Uribe family could recall. But we have suspected that this offer may have actually led to his marrying a Danish woman his mother wanted for him.

Suffice to say Emile had a huge loving Colombian family, perhaps a delightful surprise for him. It was here in South America that he learned that families can be fun and an extension of one's individual life. And it is very possible that, if the myth is true, Colombia is filled with lots of absolutely gorgeous senoritas. He told co-author Frank's family this story among many (see below). We placed it here to give a snapshot of Emile in his new milieu:

THE COLOMBIAN FUNERAL

Emile was dating a young Colombian woman, and according to proper middle-class mores, a chaperone

guy. We never found out. Emile never told us the *rest* of the story.

MORE ON EMILE'S DOMESTIC life will be added later. Right now we have to leave familial bliss to go to what really was happening in Colombia, a pall affecting all Colombians including the Gauguin-Uribe clan: *civil war.*

lead troops? Why did he wait an entire year before he joined? Why did he chose to fight for the Rebels? Which side were the Uribe's on? When did he contract malaria and was it debilitating enough to force him out of active service?

Before we try to get answers and assemble them into a whole, we need to provide some background. Indeed, a subchapter title could be "Colombia's Continuum of Civil Strife".

A BRIEF, OVERLY-SIMPLIFIED POLITICAL HISTORY OF COLOMBIA

In 1900 when Emile left the 'elderly' 377-year-old country, Denmark, claimed by some historians to have its official start in 1523, infant Colombia still in 'diapers' was only about 76 years old when Emile arrived. True, pre-Hispanic history began thousands of years in the past, and Spain in 1510 established its first permanent European settlement in Darien (then Gran Colombia, now Panama). Over five centuries Spain gradually relinquished her occupation of South America through bloody defeats at the hands of the Spanish colonists, in the case of Colombia, led by fierce and wily heroes such as Simon Bolivar and his brother-in-arms, Francisco Santander. Yet, as a country she did not gain her own true independence from Spain, creating her own government, writing rules, procedures and laws of state until 1824.

At that time the bloodshed stopped, but it did not last long. Indeed some observers might say that Colombia has been in sporadic, violent conflict within its borders up to and including

70s. Recall in Chapter 1 at Emile's birth in 1874 the Liberals won by a very large percentage of the vote. Either one side was not voting or that people were changing their minds, or the elections were rigged. http://www.infoplease.com/country/colombia.html

Causes and history of the Thousand Days War

The next major outburst was in 1895, five years before Emile arrived, when the Liberals tried unsuccessfully to unseat the Conservatives who held power for years. The rebellion was quickly put down but the frustration built and their resources and men under arms grew. A year later in 1899, the rebellion started with renewed energy which much later came to be known as the Thousand Days War. Appropriately it began in the Department of Santander presumably a Liberals stronghold near Bucaramanga. The war grew to involve the entire population of Colombia involving people of all ages including child soldiers. It is possible Emile read Danish newspaper articles about the political divisions and the armed conflict, and was already choosing sides.

With fewer soldiers and less materiel, Liberals General Rafael Uribe Uribe (a distant cousin of Pedro and Maria Elena) led the armed rebellion against the Conservative government. Recall that Emile was now in the fray during the final year. The Rebels (Liberals) initially financed by Venezuela eventually lost, claimed by some, due to the General's poor leadership in a final battle near the town of Palonegro a

The lethality of the war cannot be overemphasized. The death rate was about 0.7 percent per year. In comparison with other civil wars in the hemisphere within the century, the four-year-long, US Civil War (1861-1865), one of our bloodiest wars in US history, based on a population of 32 million, the death rate was less, 0.5 percent per year. The US war's lethality is considered high due mainly to modern weapons with outdated battle strategies combined with atrocious medical care of the wounded. Only the Mexican Revolution (1910-20) had a greater death rate, one percent per year. https://en.wikipedia.org/wiki/List_of_wars_by_death_toll

The war was memorialized in literature. Nobel Prize-winning novelist Gabriel Garcia Marquez wrote *No One Writes to the Colonel (1961)* a novel about a colonel in the Thousand Days War who is waiting for his pension. This colonel had a real-life compatriot: Emile with the same rank was also unlikely to have received a pension.

Another book that involved Colombian civil wars was also by Gabriel Garcia Marquez. *One Hundred Years of Solitude* (1970, English edition) is a widely acclaimed and wildly popular novel about many wars, often between the Liberals and Conservatives. In one sense, this book epitomizes Colombian history and the omnipresence of war. There is a good chance that you may have read this, but now would be a good time to revisit it to get the flavor of Colombian history. https://en.wikipedia.org/wiki/One_Hundred_Years_of_Solitude

might not yet become a Colombian citizen, he might not have had a choice of rank. Or he may have been too old. So the Rebels may have been his only option.

Our readings told us that no family could be aloof from the war. And that families depending on their politics had already chosen sides. If the Uribe-Gauguin's were Conservatives, and he was insensitive to their political positions, he may have riled them by joining the Rebels. This guess comes from an allusion to something he needed Maria Elena's forgiveness for in his 1938 letter. Did he go against their wishes embarrassing the family? Perhaps, they tried to convince him not to join, *it was not his war.* We know that Emile's father was a warrior, role model as a junior naval officer for France 30 years earlier. Did Emile want to be part of any 'old' war just to keep up the tradition?

After one year as a civilian, he probably became good enough in Colombian Spanish to lead men. The newspaper article noted that Emile bragged he was good at languages, most likely having had substantial linguistic training by the age of 25 in Denmark. He may have had pretty good knowledge of Spanish playing with the Uribe kids in Paris.

We are sure, as we mentioned in Chapter 1, that he may have had military and equestrian training in Denmark, too, at the Soro Academy. In support of this, there are several pictures at different ages that show him wearing what appears to be a distinctive, uniform jacket. Perhaps this training gave him the confidence and the credentials for leadership. Perhaps the High Gentleman's Club he belonged to in Copenhagen also provided this background in military horsemanship, regimental snobbery, military etiquette,

uniform made, bought a pistol and a sabre. One thing that we were sure of: he had a cavalry bridle (see below). We can surmise what happened next: when he got to the rendezvous point, was he issued rations, a weapon and ammo? He was briefed about the upcoming battle by his commanding officer, met his men, his adrenaline began to flow and history was about to be written.

The only picture (see Photographs II) of Emile in Colombia, kindly provided by Emile's grandson, Philippe Gauguin, gave us a peek at his equestrian/military history. The picture shows Emile on his horse holding his son Borge Emile in his lap. Recall Borge Emile was born in Denmark in 1911 dating the photo at about 1914. But look a little closer. Co-author Frank's friend, a cavalry expert, Jay Eby, of Prescott, Arizona noted that the horse's bridle was a European military design, possibly Danish. The lower set of reigns was to hold the horse's head down, a cavalry must. The lanyard on the bridle giving it a particular cavalry signature, namely to tether three to five horses together after the riders dismounted to fight. One of the riders in the troop would lead his and the other horses to a safer place while his colleagues would fight as infantry. This all fits Emile's claim that he was a cavalry officer during the war. The photo was according to his grandson Philippe taken in Sogamoso where his daughter Aline and son Pedro Maria were born.

MEXICAN REVOLUTION

Emile recounted war stories to others, but co-author Frank could not recall any. However Emile's daughter, Aline, did.

family in Barranquilla just to name a few requirements. But outside of the story that circulated among his modern Danish family there is no evidence elsewhere. Co-author Frank and his family never heard tell of it, he never mentioned it in his letter to Maria Elena or in his talk at the ladies club in Florida. True, a lack of evidence is not proof, but another good reason for not going was financial. As we will learn in the next chapter, he was struggling to eke out a meager living for his family with little cash to splurge on an extended trip. He had already spent a lot of money on steamship tickets for Olga and Aline. However the tale survived because it was a good one, told to grandchildren, cousins, nieces and nephews who retold it to their children.

In our minds it is unlikely that he fought in both wars. True, he had the addictive, adrenaline rush of war. A seasoned veteran he had the training, experience, and linguistic ability. And the timing was right - he had a year free from the family. He just had to fast decide, to take time off from work, and get money for a steamship ticket to Veracruz. If he did, he might have fought side-by-side with the grandfathers of Patricia, the wife of co-author Frank. This revolution gained worldwide attention and attracted volunteers from all over the World. Still, if we had to choose, we would have to say that he did not fight in Mexico.

THE POLITICAL CLIMATE IN POSTWAR COLOMBIA

After two decades Emile had lived in the US, he answered his Cousin Maria Elena Uribe's question about his friends back in

[he used the term *usufructo* that sent us scrambling to a dictionary], who did not understand the sacrifices that he and others had made in their behalf. He had risked his life for their freedom. And not just him, but other friends, now silenced. Further he felt that the concessions to the Liberals resulted in important political changes all Colombians could now enjoy. He called it a recent victory, but we guess he meant the years following the Thousand Days War when promised legislation had eventually became law.

We are not absolutely sure to which party Emile or the Uribe's belonged. It is likely that the Uribe family or at least some of them were Conservatives because of their involvement with the Conservative (and ruling) government. According to the Florida newspaper article, Emile fought for the Rebels which we assume represented the out-of-power Liberal party. In his letter he apologized to Maria Elena for unspecified actions, which made us wonder: *apologize for what?* Perhaps for his allegiance to the 'enemy' party, the Liberal party and Rebel side in the war embarrassed her and the Uribe-Gauguin family. Perhaps he hastily made angry accusations toward her or other Uribe's. The war divided the country and perhaps it divided the family, too. Further in his 1938 letter he wrote of the loss of his Conservative friends, suggesting that if he were ideologically Liberal, he at least was broadminded in his choice of friends. Perhaps his friends and his political position may have also embarrassed the Uribe family.

The differences between the two parties which we have already outlined above was complex, and for this we ask your

resulted in pillaging, looting, and death. But what led to the assassination? Another theory is that the political strife had its beginnings in the Spanish Civil War where one side represented the Church and the clergy (referred to as the Christian-Fascist group) and on the other, Communists, Socialists and Anarchists (often called the Judeo-Masonic camp). Scholars think Colombians may have feared a similar chain of events that started with suspicions between two sides: anti-clergy, Freemasonry-Liberals versus the Conservatives who supported the Catholic clergy. Spain much earlier had forbidden the construction of masonic temples in Colombia (recall Bolivar was a Freemason). And now, during La Violencia, these suspicions erupted into violent attacks by one group upon the other. For example, priests and nuns were tortured and brutally murdered because it was rumored they had huge stockpiles of guns and ammunition. The rumors were wrong, but it did not stop the pillaging and bloodshed. Historians are not certain of the death toll, some gave an upper figure of 300,000 over the ten-year period. And in addition to the bloodshed, entire villages were destroyed and tens of thousands were displaced from their land through intimidation and terrorist acts. **[Warning: the following reference is gruesome]**. http://en.wikipedia.org/wiki/La_Violencia. **[During the US Civil War in the early 1860s, Missouri had its own version of La Violencia.]** https://en.wikipedia.org/wiki/James%E2%80%93Younger_Gang

and Ambassador to France and created the safe and secure setting for the drafting of the Sitges document 'off campus' in Spain. This declaration provided the assurance and mechanism of a stable government following the La Violencia decade. His wife, Margarita Holguin Nieto (1905-1977) served as an official witness to the proceedings. http://www. britannica.com/EBchecked/topic/126016/Colombia/25342/ La-Violencia-dictatorship-and-democratic-restoration

Modern Guerilla groups

To a lesser extent armed strife continued to haunt Colombia. Armed guerilla groups on both sides during La Violencia committed most of the atrocities during the decade until they were ordered disbanded and their leaders killed. But according to articles below and personal account by co-author David not all these groups disappeared, or as some believed, eventually morphing into small, armed factions of guerillas operating in remote, mountainous regions.

For a detailed recollection here is co-author David's story when he took a bus from Bogota to Cali.

"I recalled an electrifying experience when traveling in rural Colombia. It was 1961 during the Hippy Years when a pal, Fred, and I visited Colombia. We were vacationing in Florida and on a whim we took a cheap flight to Bogota. Once there and after a week of sightseeing, enjoying the beauty of Bogota, the hospitable

with its hammering engines and the gut-sucking air pockets seemed comforting in comparison. Thinking back I imagined what it must have been like for Emile who may have built similar roads fifty some years earlier, and gained more respect for Emile's bravery."

In 1964 guerrilla organizations coalesced into two: ELN (Ejercito Liberacion Nacionale) and FARC (Fuerzas Armadas Revolucionarias de Colombia). We have read that the causes of these murderous groups were Marxist/Leninist principals and liberation theology (an expropriated a Christian movement about the struggle of the poor against the wealthy). But one cannot miss the ironies: they exploited terror killing and were largely funded by the drug trade. For further reading go to: https://en.wikipedia.org/wiki/FARC   https://en.wikipedia.org/wiki/National_Liberation_Army_(Colombia)

https://en.wikipedia.org/wiki/Liberation_theology

http://www.cfr.org/colombia/farc-eln-colombias-left-wing-guerrillas/p9272

The bloody conflict of guerrilla warfare that has been going on for over fifty years may be over at last. On Wednesday, August 24, 2016, an agreement was reached. After 4 years of negotiations between the Colombian government and the FARC, the last remaining guerilla group, reached a historic peace settlement. According to the newspapers the 52-year period of fighting would be over. Many could now celebrate the

HAVING SAID ALL THIS about civil war and violence, Colombia has made great progress in providing security and justice for its citizens. It is still the vibrant, wonderful place Emile fell in love with. Its fertile soil, plentiful water, beautiful scenery and comfortable weather make up what Colombians are proud of and love. As will be revealed in the next chapter Emile also loved this country, risked his life for Colombia, and wanted to make it his home, permanently. And, if events, described in the next chapter, had been kinder to him, Emile would have stayed, we would not have learned about his Colombian family, and this book would not have been conceived.

similar in elevation to Bogota, and legend holds it to be the origin of the sun. Although his distant cousin Cristian Perez Uribe says that now, Sogamoso has become gritty and industrial. But then, it was an intoxicatingly charming town that Emile would adopt as his own, with its delicious lifestyle, the one in which he would eventually wish to spend the rest of his days.

The trip from Bogota to Sogamoso was 125 miles (200 kilometers), and we wondered how Emile traveled there. Then, trains and autos did not exist. A road suitable for automobiles was not constructed until 1906 (at the order of President Rafael Reyes) who lived nearby in Santa Rosa de Viterbo. We have been told he imported the first car and needed a road for it **[recall it was President Reyes who knew the Uribe's and may have suggested Emile for the job]**. So we concluded that Emile's transportation was by horse.

To the modern mind, travel in the early 1900s in Colombia, requires some reflection. It was solely by horse (or mule, ox, and burro) or by foot. So, horses and horse-drawn vehicles were the fastest way to get around and do commerce. As our lives now unconsciously revolve around cars, theirs revolved around horses. Everyone simply knew how to ride them, how to care for them when they were injured or sick, how to handle them when pulling a carriage or wagon, how to judge their performance, and how to buy and sell them. This aggregation of skills, lore and knowledge was simply part of everyone's being and daily life.

Sogamoso's remoteness from the capitol city may have been for Emile one of its charms. It also meant that Emile would not be visiting the Uribe's in Bogota very often. Most likely he went by commercial stagecoach and that he trailed his horse.

emerging now, as I try to describe his character is that he was thoroughly immersed in the Colombian culture from making local guitars, learning and performing the local music, to dating the local senoritas, and to being a hard-riding vaquero who might have to escape quickly (from enemy troops or an angry father)! And sleep with one eye open for bandits or worse, assassins."
[One can imagine what a romantic, exciting image began to emerge in the mind of young Frank. He had a real live cowboy for a 'grandpa'.]

WORK

We had known from very general recollections and from the brief newspaper article in Florida that Emile worked as a civil engineer designing and building roads and railroads in Colombia. But we were fortunate to obtain much more detailed information to better complete the story of his employment from two sources. One was from Wikipedia which provided lots of small fragments of information. The other was an explosive, eyewitness account. It came to us indirectly due to the diligence of one of Emile's distant cousins, Cristian Perez Uribe-Holguin. He appealed to a colleague living in Sogamoso asking: "I am trying to help two guys write an important book on Gauguin history". His colleague performed a 'miracle' and discovered the answer to a number of our questions in the dusty, city archives, a 1944 article by Jorge Archila Reyes.

Not many people get a Wikipedia article about them, but Emile did (http://es.wikipedia.org/wiki/Emile_Gauguin).

personal attacks he might have made. He met Emile around 1916 when the action began. Emile was 42, Archila was about 25. He wrote that Emile came to Sogamoso in 1905 and was employed then by the national government to build roads. He implied Emile got the position through family influence. Archila claimed that Emile later struggled for a number of years doing odd jobs to support his growing family; but it was not enough. This must have be a time of great turmoil for Emile, wrote Archila, struggling financially, buffeted by setbacks in his early engineering jobs, scrounging for jobs in Sogamoso. Archila recalled Emile to be confident, energetic but brusque in character. He also recalled that he became very popular in Sogamoso having lots of friends. It was a time, continued Archila, for him to make friends with artists, artisans, political mavericks, and people near the boundary of 'acceptability' **[This was an interesting choice of words.]**

Road projects: According to Archila the national government wanted a road to improve the communication with the neighboring Department (state) of Casanare. This was Emile's first job that brought him to Sogamoso. Archila suspected that he obtained the post because managers favored people with foreign training. They made him the head engineer on what was called the Cravo Road project that extended eastward toward the center of the department. After several years of work in this relatively flat grazing land, Emile had arguments with local cattlemen over rights-of-way who claimed he goofed big time. The cattlemen won, and he was transferred to another road-building project in the mountainous Guantiva region northeast of Sogamoso. This time he met with problems early on because of arguments with

and at that time, Emile vowed that when he would marry, the woman had to be strong enough to carry him. Priscilla, his second wife, and he would exchange loving glances and laugh, kidding her about her strength. She was tall, only slightly shorter than Emile, but it is unlikely she could support his 200 some pounds... but just maybe. See them standing side-by-side in Photographs III.]

Railroad projects: The Fabio article indicated that in 1914 he was contracted to plan the course of a railroad between Tunja and Portachuelo which we translated from the Spanish "*fue contrado para realizer del trazado del ferrocarril*". That is all that was said, but we have interpreted this to mean that he surveyed the best route for the tracks, determined the requirements for the road bed, the percent grades, strength of trestles over water courses etc. We may have been too generous in his contract description and we don't know how much field-work versus drafting-table work was involved. Tunja, located on what is now Route 55 about 128 kilometers (80 miles) northeast of Bogota and about 64 kilometers (40 miles) southeast of Sogamoso. Both Tunja and Sogamoso are in the Department (State) of Boyaca. **[The following link will help you gain a sense of the geography http://commons.wikimedia.org/wiki/ File:Colombia_departments_spanish.png which also shows all the Departamentos de Colombia. The City, Bogota, lies in the northern part a long strip of land called Distrito Federal de Colombia within the southern part of the very large Departamento de Cundinamarca. AND: for an overall**

from native chiefs of Suamox and Mongui, intended to have churches and convents built in the territory of Granada in New Spain. The indigenous people were farmers and devoted to the Virgin of San Martin de Tours according to Franciscan Brother Guzman of Sogamoso, City of the Sun. Following Emile's departure, ironically the cathedral in which Emile, Bernal and Price labored was demolished to its foundation and rebuilt retaining all the detail to what it is today.] http://en.wikipedia.org/wiki/Sogamoso . Jorge Price will become an important name in Emile's life, and since Price came to Sogamoso long after Emile, his cathedral work with Price occurred around 1916. The length of time he spent at these jobs or if they were volunteered hours was not given, but it is possible that they may had been scattered over the entire time Emile lived there.

Author Frank recalled an instance that attests to his artisan/craft ability, that he could take scraps of wood with limited tools and make beautifully-crafted, exact replicas of Colombian folk guitars called *tiples* (TEE-plehs). Go to Photographs III. And they played beautifully. More stories about guitar making, Colombian chords and songs are in a later chapter.

Electric company project: Emile's next opportunity came in 1917, the creation of the new Sugamuxi and Tundama Electric Company (Tundama is a neighboring province of Sugamuxi where Sogamoso is situated). We know Emile helped form the company [It would not be surprising if he engineered the entire power plant.] and became its first manager. This bit of news was mentioned in reference 4 of the Wikipedia article (www.excelsio.net/2007/02/efemerides-de-febrero.html).   But

and brilliant, Olga was in a class of her own. She came from a long line associated with German royalty. **[Indeed, Emile's grandson, Philippe, has been told she was an heir to Charles the Great (Charlemagne) and even as far back as the Gallo-Roman Consul, Afranius Syagrius circa 350 AD!]**

After a time Emile, we think, began to weaken, perhaps through nagging letters from his mother. She probably felt Emile had to be convinced to marry a proper Danish girl, to stop him messing around with these 'foreign' women no matter how rich. *God knows if I will ever see my grandchildren, let alone Emile, again* she may have thought. So, Mette solved the problem. Olga would marry Emile. It may have taken Mette some convincing to get Olga on board, but she was *not* getting any younger, and Emile was so tall and so handsome. She would have wonderful children. She would convince Emile to return home. A simple plan and it worked. He returned to Denmark and he was introduced to his future wife. At 26 Olga must have been a dish to have won Emile's heart; and after a brief courtship, in September 10, 1908 Emile and Olga married in Frederiksberg, Denmark. See Emile in the cover photograph with the caption on page v and Olga in Photographs III.

Now for Emile came the biggest sales effort of his career. He had to convince Olga how beautiful Colombia was, how she would fall in love with it, how wonderful his Colombian family was. She was in love with her man - big, powerful, intelligent, and she knew in her heart that it was the right decision. It would be a wonderful adventure. She and Emile would conquer the World, their love so great. And if she did not like it, she

environment. We know from Emile's 1938 letter that his mother visited them in Colombia and we can be pretty sure that Mette came to be with Olga during the last part of her pregnancy, to help out and to see her new granddaughter.

In the 1938 letter Emile wrote that his mother arrived wearing a feathered cape as if she were going to attend Montezuma's palace. Emile made his humorous observation to her, but she did not think it funny and berated him for it as well as his "mocking her lack of knowledge of history and geography". She probably had no clue on Colombia's location or history or the strenuous Barranquilla-Bogota trip before she left Denmark. When she returned to Copenhagen, her humiliation was still fresh because Emile heard about it years later from his brothers who took her side.

We can only guess when Mette returned to Denmark, but it is possible that she stayed on, enjoying her granddaughter and daughter-in-law and the beautiful, exotic location. We also know that she was acquainted with and visited with the wife of the French Ambassador in Bogota. This friendship was rather deep because Mette gave her a small watercolor landscape by husband, Paul. Painted in 1875 it was freely-done, in bright colors featuring a country church. We all assume that Mette brought it with her when she visited Olga and Emile. She wrote a very personal note on the back of the work, addressed to the Ambassador's wife, Maria Mancini. Eventually the painting was given to Maria Elena, who then gave it to Cristian Perez Uribe-Holguin's mother Emilia Perez. Cristian noted that it was confirmed to be an authentic Gauguin, and it was finally sold to Banco de la Republica.

The diary goes on to say that Olga had tired of her marriage and Colombia, and her mom went to console her. We imagine that Emile did a lot of pleading, too. *Yes, there would be no more pregnancies, yes, he would get steady work, and yes, they would plan for their future in Denmark.* The conciliation worked ... for three years.

FAILURE TO RECONCILE - BREAKUP NUMBER ONE

Olga who may have had in the back of her mind a short duration in Sogamoso now feared it might become a lifetime. Olga, a beautiful, genteel-looking woman, we will learn was one tough gal who was not afraid to make tough decisions. She must have been continually nagging Emile to get out of there. And she was even more emphatic now that they almost lost Pedro Maria. **[Ironically a non-hygienic hospital in 'first-World' Denmark is what killed Emile's brother.]** But leaving would be difficult. Because of Emile's sporadic employment, paying for steamship tickets would not be easy. Also war with Germany (1914-1918) was raging in Europe, and although Colombia and Denmark were not directly involved, German U-Boats were making oceanic travel dangerous, sinking many commercial ships including the British passenger ship the *Lusitania* in May 19, 1915. But that did not deter Olga's desire to depart. Olga made a list of her horrible experiences that together would seal her decision, which in his 1938 letter Emile recounted to his Cousin Maria Elena.

Despite the near tragedy in the delivery room, the parents were joyous with their new child. We guess the name Pedro Maria was chosen to honor his two cousins, Pedro and Maria Elena, perhaps as memorial to the wonderful times they did have together there. This might seem strange to us first, because there is so little evidence that they socialized with the Uribe's in Bogota, and that the name 'Maria' was associated with the Virgin Mary an anathema to Danes particularly to Olga. But it was chic in Europe at the time: for example, 'Carl Maria von Weber', the German composer. Yet despite his ragged start, Pedro Maria went on to greater things in his life as a soldier-of-fortune, author and a career at a high level in law enforcement. See Photographs I for him among other family members in a family reunion portrait.

The next reason Olga wanted out was schooling. Emile told Maria Elena an amusing anecdote that occurred when Olga blamed the school not providing a good education for her kids. Pedro Maria was having trouble forming words and sentences in school producing instead incomprehensible grunts. But outside the school he had no trouble pronouncing swear words and vulgar expressions with perfect enunciation.

Another reason for Olga's eagerness to depart was she felt she was not respected. One incident occurred when her servants did not give her or her property due fealty. [**After all she did have royalty in her veins.**] One night Olga awoke to find that the cook was wearing one of her favorite camisoles embroidered with an ornate monogram "O von H" and if that was not enough of an insult, her housemaid entered wearing another camisole with

Her granddaughter Mette Fonseca Gauguin poignantly summarized Olga's frustration and bitterness that Emile, the optimist, was continually like the other Gauguin males seeking greatness, and she allowed him to "drag her and the family through his adventures" (see her last entry in Family Comments in the Appendix).

The attempt at reconciliation was in ruin. And Emile's happiness must have been at its lowest, too. But wait! His life was in Colombia and he, too, was adamant. He was a citizen. This was his home. He had great skills and he could get work any time.

And we will learn he will soon have a great position, but more than a job it will be something he could do for the city of Sogamoso. And its citizens would sing his praise. And he would win Olga back.

THE JOB OF A LIFETIME

The big fight with Olga and her departure with the kids must have put any husband and father into a depressing tail spin. But not Emile. His philosophy was: when one door closes, another opens. And shortly his philosophy prevailed – another door did open.

A sudden opportunity arose: a new electric company was formed **[possibly by Emile, but we could not find out who actually was the creator]** which launched him into a new high. As usual 'all was not lost' he must have thought. It was fantastic. It was the best thing yet that happened to him. There

manager, a Mr. Calderon, giving the situation a dramatic tone.] The revolt worked for the shareholders including the American company, General Electric Corp. The present owner voted in a new board to reform the company. But that meant new elections and new officers.

This time, in a matter of months, Emile's luck ran out; his winnings became his losses. He lost the election to a newly arrived gentleman, Jorge Price, from Bogota **[His fellow artisan who turned out to be his arch nemesis.]**; and Emile was forced out after a second vote, presumably to break a tie: the final humiliating blow. Archila concluded that the situation in the meeting in a local patrician's mansion had high drama. Dr. Gauguin, according to Archila, was assured to be reelected, but when the final votes were counted the color of Emile's face drained. Of the 400 votes cast only 120 went to Dr. Gauguin. For reasons unknown his friends and supporters went to the newcomer, Dr. Jorge Price. The legal representatives Mr. Roberto Wesselhoeft and John Wisner, the main shareholders of the company at first went to Emile to show their support but during the second round, Dr. Price became the new manager.

Archila said that Emile rose like an automaton, shocked that his supporters and friends had virtually stabbed him in the back, and like a zombie, his face red with humiliation he stumbled from the meeting before it was concluded, straight to the office where he began to make everything ready for the new manager.

Thus, the cofounder of the company, the one whose leadership and hard work developed it, was now through devious and

It seemed to us that Emile was sandbagged by Sogamosan cronies. It's no wonder Emile wanted to clear out of this den of false friends and duplicitous colleagues. True, he left behind lots of true friends and memories, and according to Archila, Emile returned to Colombia several times supporting our guess that he developed a friendship with his much younger cousin Blanca Williamson. If this is any consolation, Emile outlived Price by two years, and no one wrote a Wikipedia article about Price or Archila. But the big point here is that if Emile had not been betrayed, it is very likely he would never have become co-author Frank's virtual grandfather and this book would never have been written. When one door closes, another will open.

With his pride destroyed, he followed a year later (not to Denmark as Archila wrote), but to the United States. We wondered if Emile returned first to Bogota to say his 'goodbyes'. Probably, not. The situation likely was too embarrassing. His avoidance of a final visit may have prompted his mysterious apology to Maria Elena 11 years later.

We knew that Emile loved Colombia, we knew that he had just gotten a great offer, we knew that he had many friends in Sogamoso who loved and respected him. Giving up on his marriage with Olga, at least temporarily, was counteracted by already having a truly wonderful, vigorous, and powerful family in Colombia. We surmised that the reasons for leaving Denmark in the first place were still painfully fresh. And for that reason we knew that he was not going back to Denmark even though that it meant giving up on his own family.

to the trash-filled Danish sea cynically alluding to the Danish national anthem.

But it was not his war buddies, *companeros de la guerra* (who called him 'Don Emilio' or 'El Colonel') who could vote for him, but blaggards at the 'height of respectability' whose votes he needed, people unappreciative of his sacrifice who did not smell the gun smoke and the stench of death, or hear the thunder of guns and the cries of the injured.

REGARDLESS OF ANY UNANSWERED speculations about the loss of his beloved Colombia and the loss of his little children, we have to depart Colombia with Emile, despite his eloquent yearning to stay, to leave this colorful adventure. As we will learn later, his behavior in the US was to work hard but eschew wealth, position and status there, too. Perhaps, he knew when to walk away from the 'game', when to fold. Cash in your chips and mosey on. Maybe it was his habitual inability to hold a job, to resist conformity at the cost of unemployment. Maybe it was simply to avoid getting burned again. But we believe that Emile's subliminal goal was that of his great-grandmother, Flora Tristan, to leave the game of life, making us all a little richer with no financial profit for themselves.

EMILE MEETS AXEL

He looked down from the gangplank and saw a guy with a round face set off by a small mustache and round spectacles to match his face. Axel recognized him, too. Who wouldn't? *A giant is hard to hide*, Axel cackled to himself. He recognized him from the photograph. Definitely it was Axel Malm, his new boss really did come all the way from Philadelphia to meet him. Wow. What a feeling of finally being wanted!

After going through immigration and customs there was Axel again. This time they were hugging and backslapping. Axel's rasping laugh and "How are you old man?" He had a porter take care of shipping his trunk to an address in Philadelphia, then they went outside, climbed into a cab and headed for Penn Station. The griminess of New York and the oppressive August heat and humidity did not bother him. He was too busy emerging into the excitement of the Manhattan scene and his new friend and boss. Axel was paying for everything in US dollars, peeling them off from a large roll of bills, the World-famous greenbacks. More money than he had seen in years. This was his kind of town. This was his kind of country.

Axel had already bought his ticket, now he bought lunch. Emile probably had a corned beef sandwich on rye and a Cel Ray soda, at a corner delicatessen across the street from the station. It was new and strange yet it was all too familiar. What a feeling! And that Jewish food was delicious.

Axel told him that Pennsylvania Station was finished seven years ago. He marveled at the newness of it and imagined the

indecision on his part. Denmark and Colombia were far in the past. Here was his new home, his final destination. A lot of immigrants postpone this step of permanently giving up one's homeland. But not Emile.

Appendicitis.

No sooner had he began to settle down in his new room with the Samper-Barrigas family, he became very sick with terrible abdominal pain so intense he went to a hospital. The family was Spanish-surnamed perhaps Colombian, he may have known about before he left. Emile wrote in his 1938 letter that they "were very fine with me" when he first arrived. We think that with the change in diet and the stress of unhappy departure from Colombia he became ill with acute appendicitis. But not only was he becoming very sick in his newly adopted country, he had little money to pay medical bills. In his 1938 letter Emile describes to Maria Elena his encounter with the hospital staff. When he told them that the price was too high, they said for him to talk with Dr. Mattheus, the surgeon. The front office disobeyed all protocol sending him right to the surgeon office. Confronted, the administrator indignantly told him it was impossible and showed Emile to the door. But in the hubbub, the surgeon walked in asking Emile what he wanted. Emile blurted out what he would charge for an appendectomy. The doctor asked his nationality, "Are you from Scandinavia?" Emile told him that he was French. **[Up until now we have incorrectly assumed Emile thought of himself as Danish. Sorry.]**

Recall his relationship with Olga was already bleak. Fresh in her mind were many negatives. She could never forget almost losing Pedro Maria in childbirth in an unsanitary hospital or the oppressive effect of Catholicism on her daughter and probably the same fate would await the boys. Also she could not stand the plebian nature of Sogamoso and her uppity servants were always snickering behind her back. She never knew how long Emile could stay employed. No, Olga threw in the sponge on Colombia, her marriage, and Emile.

But Emile must have sent some impressive letters to change her mind. We guess the length of time away from Emile had an effect, too. He may have suggested he yearned for her kisses. And finally, in the end, he convinced her to come back to him and stay, that things would get better, that he had a really great job with a steady income and status. After all, the US was more advanced economically, it was safer and closer to Denmark. In any case she decided to give it a try. We will call this 'Reconciliation II'.

Emile's 1938 letter to Maria Elena said that two months after his recuperation from surgery he obtained a well-paying government position. He was already employed by Malm Engineering, but we surmised that this was not regular work. **[Curiously he never mentioned to Maria Elena his position with Malm Engineering]**. His finances began to improve enough to carry out his long-term plan: to bring his family here and make a home for them in the US, and he asked Olga, her mother and the children to come to the US. Ostensibly, getting his feet on the ground financially with a steady, well-paying

Still, there must have been lots of hugs and kisses after two long years. Finally they were together again, united like old times. A family again. Bliss.

Deep down, Olga still loved Emile the father of her children who loved their daddy, and she wanted them to have a father. Yet she had strong reservations about living in the US. Perhaps Olga wanted her mother to stay with them if she agreed to move. Perhaps she needed a biased opinion. But she definitely needed at least a little family in this foreign, hostile land, and she needed a babysitter if she were to give undivided attention to the negotiations.

He rented a house Atlantic City and was earning $100 per month. [**We wondered why he chose Atlantic City. Perhaps he felt the gray, fall skies and ocean would make the family feel they were back home.**] But after a while the lack of servants, family and friends got to them. They all felt that the US was very unfriendly. This was not good for Emile who was trying to convince Olga the US was the right move.

Despite these difficulties, Emile and Olga began working on their reconciliation and things were going well ... until Emile was fired. As the money began to run out Olga and her mom began to panic. Was this the old Emile whose big mouth and irrepressible brusqueness that kept him from having a steady income in Colombia? They could not imagine living without servants and they did not find the US, particularly Atlantic City, to be very hospitable. Emile acquiesced, so they moved to a house in Philadelphia. But eventually they

documents. Emile, explaining all the drama and callous deception to his cousin, told her that now they were as good as murdered as far as he was concerned. From then on, to him, his family was virtually dead.

Olga and her mother with children in hand departed for Denmark in mixed triumph and sadness. In that two-year period of yearning for his wife and kids, Emile had become soured on the family, suddenly, abruptly, and irreversibly. In the retelling to his cousin this tragic account maintaining the drama, the details and his humiliating defeat and loss were still painfully vivid in his mind 20 years later. We will have to wait until 1935 for the next act of this family pageant.

Our guess was that Olga had no intention of staying, and with Emile's seeming intractability about refusing to return to Denmark and his intense, and 'foolish' commitment to be an American, it was all apparent. Her marriage was hopeless. Homeward bound tickets were purchased for departure and on April 23, 1919 (the US Immigration stamp on Olga's passport) she and her family departed from New York arriving May 5th in Copenhagen. Facing a wondering family at the dock, Olga walked down the steamship's gangplank empty-handed, broken-hearted, humiliated and infuriated. She must have had this consoling thought: *Like father, like son.*

Mette Gauguin Fonseca gave us a curious document, dated April 9, 1919, hand-written about two weeks before Olga departed for Denmark stating that Emile agreed to pay half of

MARIE GAUGUIN DE URIBE AND THE SPANISH INFLUENZA PANDEMIC

Amid all the family drama another far more serious even cataclysmic drama was in motion, indeed it was one of the most incredible events in the 20th Century, Biblical in its proportions: the Spanish Flu. In the midst of these swirling, distasteful, family details as momentous as they were to the teetering young Gauguin family, the entire World including the US, Colombia and Denmark from 1917 to 1920 was gripped in a raging pandemic of biological terror.

When Emile left Colombia for the US, the Spanish Influenza Epidemic was about to infect 500 million and according to some reports (Wikipedia) kill 40-100 million people worldwide, the death rate peaking in 1918 and decreasing until 1920. The worst medical holocaust in recorded history, killing 3-5 percent of the World population - more people in one year than the Black Death did in four.

To the best of our knowledge no one in the Gauguin-Uribe families reported to us that the pandemic affected them. But our research revealed there was one death in the family during that grim period: that of Paul's sister, Marie Gauguin de Uribe. She died in 1918 at age 71, Could the cause have been the Spanish Flu?

THE AMERICA EMILE WOULD HAVE KNOWN

To give an idea as to what the US was like when Emile debarked onto the docks of New York City, in 1917 President

Whether or not Emile was aware of all this was unknown. When he stepped off the boat WWI was over and the ensuing decade grew into what has come to be called the Roaring Twenties an enormous cultural change from rural Colombia. True, staid, conservative Philadelphia, New York City's largest and most boring 'suburb', was probably the least roaring place.

But before these 'roaring years', three years after coming to the land of opportunity, Emile found himself in the midst of a depression, The Forgotten Depression, 1.5 years long, but still serious with unemployment tripling to almost 9 percent, the Dow Jones Average (a quick metric of stock value and economy status) losing half its value from a high of 60. Malm Engineering must have felt the pinch, but it was nothing compared to what lay in store.

MORE ON GAUGUIN HISTORY

On September 27, 1920, Emile's mother, Mette Sophie Gad Gauguin, died in Copenhagen at age 70. We have no indication that Emile traveled home for the funeral. Much later in 2007 co-author David and his wife, Lois, visited Copenhagen and met Paul's great-grandson, Clovis Gauguin and Emile's grandson, Philippe Gauguin and his wife, Helle. They took them to visit Mette's grave site. Her grave marker does not mention her husband, Paul Gauguin, who was, at the time of her death, world famous. She had the last word...for eternity!

Although Emile may not have gone to his mother's funeral, he did not stop being Paul Gauguin's son. In 1921, Emile from

of corruption died suddenly in office, but during that time and after, Emile witnessed many eye-popping events take place. Months before Harding's election no doubt aided by the Nineteenth Amendment to the Constitution ratified in 1920 (after a 30-year battle) allowing women to vote for the first time in the history of the US. In Denmark wheels of progress turned more quickly: Emile's wife and mother already could vote in 1915, but Colombia remained a male-only bastion until 1954. While the US finally granted freedom to vote to half the population, it restricted the immigration of Eastern Europeans. And although the US did not ratify the anti-German Versailles Treaty, we in September of 1922 did ratify severe trade tariffs which helped set off an economic boom in the US that further fueled the Roaring Twenties but, as an unintended consequence, also blamed by many to have helped Hitler's rapid rise to power.

The ban of the sale of alcoholic beverages continued (until the 18th Amendment was repealed in 1933). Although the country was 'dry', the people tried all means including illegal ones to have a drink or two at secret bars (or even get drunk), at watering places nicknamed speakeasies and blind pigs. Humorist Will Rogers was known to have said Americans wanted prohibition as long as they could still stagger to the polls to vote for it. This was an odd law for the Roaring Twenties. To Emile, this was of no importance. His 1938 letter states in several places he never drank.

Emile most likely read newspapers, but radio was a possibility, too. Regardless of which media he used we do know that he

elect this seemingly, low-key person to offset the country's excesses. This biography is also a highly recommended history of the US at the time, published at the same time Emile wrote his epic letter, is available free online. White implied the US populace loved Coolidge's conservatism while enjoying the exhilarating economic and social whirlwind.

Americans would also enjoy Mount Rushmore. Coolidge in 1927 provided matching funds to have Danish-American Gutzon Borglum to begin to carve the heads of four American presidents in the rock outcroppings of Mount Rushmore in the Black Hills of South Dakota. Borglum, the son of the second wife of a Mormon father, did not continue being a Latter Day Saint and studied sculpture with August Rodin in France. https://en.wikipedia.org/wiki/Gutzon_Borglum http://www.pbs.org/wgbh/americanexperience/features/biography/rushmore-borglum/

JEAN GAUGUIN IMPORTED SCULPTURES STORY
Another Danish sculptor who also appeared on the scene during the 1920s was Emile's brother, Jean. Emile in his 1938 letter, amusingly recounted his attempts to import Jean's works into the US. Jean, he wrote, imported a lot and sold a lot, too. He has a beautiful fountain made of porcelain in the Luxembourg Gardens in Paris, but Jean did not like it: too calm. He wrote convincingly the need for movement in some statues. Yet for the fountain, it required calm. He made a series of bullfight

he still had a large circle of lucrative contacts in the art world likely because of his last name.]

In a recent email Emile's grandson Philippe added these clarifications: "The period 1890-1945 was indeed inspired by Greek art in Denmark. Danish art in this period is, by the way, very impressive, too. Ironically it seems that modern Greeks call Copenhagen 'Athens of the North'. And as for my great uncle, Jean Gauguin, I have seen many of his works. Go to https://www.kulturarv.dk/kid/VisKunstner.do?kunstnerId=253   for a few examples, but no bullfight or baseball examples."

EMILE TOLD MARIA ELENA MORE ABOUT HIS FAMILY

Emile's long, 1938 letter to Maria Elena covered many topics, perhaps in answer to questions she raised in previous letters to him. One of the topics involved his mother and brothers. The tone of Emile's feelings toward his brothers ranged from angry jealousy to unwilling respect. Angry at them for trying to take advantage of their father's fame (recall we have already quoted Emile's smug pride ingenuously claiming he never profited from his father's success) and as a result, feeling that they too should share his sentiments, but at the same time complimenting their successes in art and literature in their careers.

Emile had mercilessly kidded his mother when she visited him in Colombia about her 'Montezuma-style feathered cape'

the Nobel Prize in Literature, and Edvard lived in the North
and was famous as a dramatist and a financier. Ernst did not
make as big a name for himself because he committed suicide
at age 48. Emile added that he was like Ernst: more intelligent than his brothers, with few accomplishments, and as good
as dead. [**This detailed knowledge of Emile's revealed that
he was far more interested in family details than he let on
to be. Philippe Gauguin, Emile's grandson, confirmed
the genealogy. Note also that Emile seemed to be drawing
a parallel: he was smarter and less accomplished than his
own brothers. But as good as dead. Was Emile trying to
tell Maria Elena he was suicidal? Ernst, on the contrary,
trained as an economist, was a very accomplished writer,
social critic, journalist and publisher. He was falsely fined
and imprisoned for religious blasphemy. Despondent, he
killed himself with poison. https://en.wikipedia.org/wiki/
Ernst_Immanuel_Cohen_Brandes**]

THE AMERICA EMILE WOULD HAVE KNOWN (CONT.)

In 1928 when straight-laced, self-made millionaire presidential
candidate Herbert Hoover stated "We in America today are
nearer to the final triumph over poverty than ever before in the
history of any land" and crushed Al Smith an affable, New York
Catholic associated with Tammany Hall corruption scandals in
the presidential election extending the Republican hold on the
presidency for another four years until 1933. The promise "a

because one of the proposed sites was near Boulder Canyon, the Democrats bitterly and tenaciously resisted for years any attempt to have it renamed after the person who originated the idea for its construction. Also, his signature in 1931 made *The Star-Spangled Banner* our official national anthem.

WHETHER OR NOT HE voted for Hoover, Emile was about to experience the American Great Depression in an intense, iconic and personal way.

In a fit of anger and discouragement he burned all the paintings. He also admitted to Maria Elena that he cried during the process. [**Emile, the painter, came as a complete surprise to us. Co-author Frank saw only one piece of work of Emile's that one could call a painting - a large, color cartoon, rather crude, wooden-looking without art or style, meant to be funny but wasn't. It was thrown away by Frank's mother – a work of a Gauguin. The only picture of his surviving artwork is in Photographs III. Using a pen and ink he decorated the wood surface of an empty, thread spool with indigenous designs. Was this the genre of the paintings he burned? Or were they cartoons?**]

He said 'goodbye' to the owners of the house where he had lived, and packed into his car what he could not give away or sell. That must have included some clothes, cooking gear, a book or two, maps, surveying tools (see Photographs III), and some food and headed out on what he called the *Camino Real*.

Why Emile chose this name we may never know, but it has an interesting history. According to Wikipedia any road built under the jurisdiction of the Spanish Crown was called *Camino Real* or royal road. In Mexico and perhaps all of South America there were actual roads traveled by aboriginal kings. It is also the name of a recent chain of hotels mainly in Mexico. In California it is the name of the 600 mile (922 kilometer) stretch of road connecting the 21 missions from San Diego to San Francisco, then called *El Camino Real*. The missions built under the leadership of Brother Junipero Serra date back

a name that lent dignity to the humility of poverty. Although composed years later, it might be the spirit that Roger Miller captured in *King of the Road*. If you have not heard this great song, check it out on YouTube or **http://www.songfacts.com/ detail.php?id=7480**. You will feel Emile's desperation when he had no money for cigarettes.

There is another song that evokes the ghost of Emile: Woody Guthrie's, *The Greatest Thing that Man Has Ever Done: The Great Historical Bum* about a mythical, super hero working his way through history from the beginning of human kind building the Rock of Ages to working in World War II defense plants,

https://www.youtube.com/watch?v=qB-YnV0e3Lc

http://woodyguthrie.org/Lyrics/Biggest_Thing_That_ Man.htm A topic that might speak to the labor movement that was just beginning in the US and the nobility of the common worker, was curiously championed over a hundred years earlier by Emile's great-grandmother, Flora Tristan.

Emile went on to describe his travels in search for work writing that he crossed the US up and down and back and forth so many times his tracks would have looked like a map of a city the size of the entire country. He went from New York City to San Francisco, from Lake Superior to Hermosillo, Mexico. He built roads in the mountains of New Mexico at 3,000 meters (9,800 feet) where the snow was 50 centimeters (20 inches) deep. He worked as an accountant in Arizona where the temperature reached 43° C (almost 110° F). He had a job in a gold mine in California that was 2500 meters (8,200 feet) deep. The atmosphere was so bad there he had to go to the elevator to

money home and not be a burden on their impoverished parents. The government set up homeless shelters that provided clothes, food and tobacco for $2 a day, but in Emile's view, 2 million decent people preferred to chop wood for meals rather than take handouts. Over those years he held in great honor these people and contempt for those on the dole. **[Emile's political position suggested to us that he did not favor the social programs in Roosevelt's New Deal. He was not the only one. For a broader view of that time there are many fine books available such as Terkel (1987) and Brinkley (2016) under References.]** He noted that people were stoically bearing this setback with the faith it would not last forever. He must have been writing about his plight to others, because he feared he would be boring his audience, saying that he would stop telling the saga of his bankruptcy.

Emile's *Camino Real* story paused briefly and unfortunately because we would have loved that he told his cousin more, but he had a date to reconcile with Olga and his children, *next*, after a few more Depression stories.

OTHER DEPRESSION STORIES

At various places in the book we guessed about Emile's political leanings. For example, his rant against government aid would make him a Republican, and many Americans then, hated their president because he was making it too easy with expensive government programs. Regarding Emile's objections we can guess where his sympathies lay. But on the Democrat's side, President

to resemble a ghost town, perhaps Frank's colleague's idea will have more sway.

Because one had to be unmarried and between the ages of 18-25, Emile did not work in this program nor did many other 'kings of the road' who were on their own *Camino Real*. But according to Uys, over a 10-year period, at least 2.5 million youths participated. And he quoted one person saying that the CCC and the Works Progress Administration (WPA) prevented an armed revolution. Uys' authoritative book is a 'must read' for those interested in the topic (go to References).

PARK-BENCH BUMS AND LOAN COLLECTORS

Here is another Emile tale that took place before co-author Frank met him that involved his boss Axel Malm. Recall Malm Engineering went broke back in the mid-20s and we are not sure when it did reopen. So, both Emile and Axel were in all likelihood in an extreme need of money just to satisfy their daily needs. This tale likely took place sometime during these dark days perhaps when Emile returned periodically from the *Camino Real*.

> "It started [**as co-author Frank recalled from Emile's stories often repeated in the family**] when President Malm and his top guy (and maybe only guy) Vice President Gauguin became desperate. They had reached bottom financially. They both were sitting on a park bench in Philadelphia one day, strategizing their dismal future, when *bang!*, a light bulb went off in their heads. They decided on a scheme. They bought 100,

Cleveland themselves struggling to make a living after graduating from high school to have a major effect on the similarly afflicted multitude by creating a person dedicated to providing 'truth, justice and the American way'. This was just what the US needed and maybe even Danes in Denmark and Colombians in Colombia, a hero, a deliverer from the poverty, uncertainty and eventually the horrors of the Second World War. Ironically they created a billion dollar industry, but even more ironically, through bad contract negotiation ended up themselves, penniless. Their names were Joe Shuster and Jerry Siegel; their creation, Superman.

Frank's Uncle Donald, likely a member of the top '1 percent' who never knew hunger, a sophisticated gynecologist living on fashionable Beacon Hill in downtown Boston loved to listen to the radio program, *The Adventures of Superman* during World War II. Despite his wealth he saw the benefits of truth and justice. It was a popular panacea for many at all levels of US life then. It is hard to believe that Axel and Emile did not hear of this amazing superhero, let alone read Superman comics or listen to the program. Maybe they used him as a role model to justify collecting unpaid loans from profiteers and corrupt businessmen as Superman did. Or were they just plain thugs?

A CLOSER LOOK AT THE CRASH, DEPRESSION, AND RECOVERY

The Dow Jones Average more specifically is a price-weighted average of 60 blue-chip, industrial stocks chosen by the editors

their lives in a country with so much promise but so little to give. Still Emile reported from his travels across North America and his visits at hobo camps there was great optimism for a recovery which had not occurred yet.

Officially, now, one can view it more technically. National output according to Wikipedia fell by one-third and hence, wide unemployment went to 25 percent. This compared to an average rate of 5 percent during normal times which rarely went as high as 9 percent for the rest of the 20th Century. But these numbers don't tell the full story because a third of the employed only worked part time. And all received smaller paychecks. There was deflation with price drops of 20 percent, good news for the unemployed and under employed as their money went further, but at the government level it had a wide ripple effect making it difficult paying off national debt. The root cause thought by some was the Smoot-Hawley Tariff Act of 1930 that increased the cost of imports having unintended consequences of limiting growth and stymieing the economy. This encouraged other countries into a tariff war that many economists believe contributed to the downward, spiraling effect extending the depth and duration of the global depression impacting people in all countries including Denmark, particularly Emile's children whose father could barely support himself (see the email comments by some of his grandchildren in the Appendix.)

The convergence of other factors combined to increase the problem. For instance the absence of margin requirements in the stock market, allowing investors to borrow money without

we take for granted today. She created the 40 hour work week and a minimum wage. She instituted a ban on child labor and established a national retirement plan, Social Security. She produced a workers compensation plan for those injured on the job. It took her just 12 years.

These landmark changes revolutionized American life and wellbeing, and in some quarters raised the cry of Socialism. Although Emile we can guess was an opponent of Roosevelt's plans, he was going to marry one of his products, Priscilla. Of course he had not met her yet, his jobless bride-to-be Priscilla Buntin, ironically was later employed successively by two of Roosevelt's New Deal programs.

The American Great Depression was a major and compelling theme in this book, but another was a series of episodes about Emile's struggle for *and* with his family: the one that follows was Act III of the reconciliation attempt of Olga and Emile.

RECONCILIATION: ACT III

Emile continued giving Maria Elena his news update in his long, 1938 letter. He told her that a Danish painter, after being celebrated in Paris exhibited her paintings in 1934 in Philadelphia. She was told that another Danish person, son of the great Paul Gauguin, lived in Philadelphia. She tried to look Emile up but only found the 'ashes' of his burned 'masterpieces'. The son of his foster parents, probably Pier Malm, did show her a sketch that escaped the bonfire. After returning to Denmark she made

When he arrived to Copenhagen, he was treated like royalty. Their children were grown. Borge Emile had finished an engineering degree in Germany, Pedro Maria had become a professional painter, and Aline was married with a small but frail daughter. Emile really liked his impressive son-in-law. And, Emile was happy too. In typical Emile fashion, he found a job in construction.

The first days read like a romantic novel or a sonnet of love. Olga was missing his kisses and caresses. Everything was returning to normal. Happiness was everywhere - except for one thing. Emile was unable to satisfy his amorous Olga. After a number of rejections, an explosion was about to happen.

But upon closer inspection, all was not back to normal. His children overly optimistic set up a double bed, despite Emile's protests. Olga even at 52, felt she still had it – all the curves in the right places. She craved her man - and what a man he was. She was horny. Emile in Sogamoso and Philadelphia could satisfy his bride. Each time he renewed their love after tempestuous arguments with torrid make-up sex. But now he was lifeless. What had happened? Many questions kept recurring. Was it him? Or did he want a 'newer model'? True, they were now almost strangers, and their 17-year absence made her more desirous. But now perhaps she felt Emile had become simply a docile bull. What had happened to his ability to make ferocious love? Perhaps she really did not truly absolve herself of her sins and wrongs. Perhaps she was still skeptical of the old Emile. Perhaps she still was unable to stifle her rage that was still there.

he hates drunks, but this time he loved them. Their generous tips shortened his stay.

A 1935 UPDATE ON HIS BROTHERS JEAN AND POLA

Emile's trip back to Denmark was not a complete loss. He told Maria Elena about his brother Jean's success as a sculptor and his life, but his resentment showed by calling him a fool (after the saying, 'fools rush in where angels fear to tread', implying that he, Emile, is the angel). He also refused to visit with him socially during Reconciliation III using the excuse that he did not drink and would have been unable to pay him back.

Emile asserted that Jean had made a name for himself, better known by the masses than his father, concluding that he was wise not to be a painter. Emile sarcastically wrote that he was referred to as Sir Sculptor Jean Gauguin of Copenhagen with his picture in the Danish Encyclopedia. Emile felt he had the same temperament as his dad but the same physical face as his mom. Jean divorced and remarried and produced a one-year-old. Emile praised his vitality. But then wrote that his brother had few interests except reading popular chemistry books and learning languages. It seemed baffling to us that Emile claimed Jean was also a lawyer periodically specializing in cases against the police. Emile had grudging respect for him but could not resist a nasty, concluding remark, saying Jean thought of himself as a lion, but really was only a mouse. [**We are guessing this bitterness about his brothers was a severe case of sibling**

publishing the book about his dad, published the personal correspondence between Paul and Mette, to the embarrassment of his mother's memory. Emile noted that he wrote a scathing reply to Pola, still upset by Pola's criticism of his teasing their mom about her Montezuma cape. [**Clearly Pola was critical of Emile's treatment of their mother, but was Pola critical of his mother, too?**]

Mette Fonseca Gauguin had two recollections about her grandfather Emile's visit to Denmark with the sad and depressing outcome of Reconciliation III. First, she learned that her grandmother, Olga, filed for divorce immediately after Emile departed. The other was one of Emile's zingers.

> "Hi Emile", his mother-in-law called out when she saw him after all those years. "You look much older."
>
> Emile, without missing a beat answered, "You look much heavier."

EMILE RETURNS

The steamship *Manhattan* docked in New York on February 18, 1937 arriving from Hamburg, Germany with passenger, Emile Gauguin, who returned to his home on 4312 Chestnut Street (this could be where the Samper-Barrigas family lived or the Malm's). It was just a few blocks from where co-author Frank lived while in graduate school, a street in West Philadelphia lined on both sides with huge, four story houses some of which were converted to apartments, some had extended families who

Then, he added a curious thought: he saluted the 'wandering Jew', Ahasuerus.

We were so impressed with his knowledge of biblical history and legend, we did a little checking. [**His use of the name Ahasuerus is an allusion to a 13th Century tale of the man who taunted Jesus on the way to his crucifixion, and as punishment had to wander, homeless and scavenging until the second coming of Jesus. Emile in several places in his letter praised Jews and his love for them. It is no wonder that he saw Ahasuerus as a soul mate. Coincidently, Nazi Germany recently passed the Nuremburg Laws depriving German Jews of their civil rights. The Ahasuerus story perhaps had its start when it was indirectly mentioned in Matthew 16:28 (KJV). To add to the topic it was a name applied to the Persian king Xerxes I. More of its rich history is in https:// en.wikipedia.org/wiki/Wandering_Jew. Incidentally, it was an expression used in 19th Century Mexico, *El Judio Errante* referring to someone who moved around a lot, and perhaps in Emile's time in Colombia where he may have first heard the term. Finally, Wandering Jew is a flowering plant of the spiderwort family or genus Tradescantia of cytogenetic significance.**]

EMILE'S EMBASSY VISITS FOR COLOMBIA
UPDATES
Despite his bad memories of Colombia he still missed its charms. Emile yearned to find out about Colombia in general,

and instead asked her to produce someone who knew his Colombian family and Sogamosan pals. He specified an expert on Bogota. With only a short wait, out stepped a young man dressed so elegantly he would have been ready for a wedding with royalty, someone who might have appeared on the cover of a fashion magazine. But with a chest so proud it deserved at least a couple of Cordobas, Emile wondered. [**Emile was referring to the Medal for Valor named for Colombian Army's General Jose Maria Cordoba**].

Emile concluded (paraphrasing): *He would have liked to have had a broader conversation with this popinjay but he was unable to bring him down from his pedestal. Emile realized that this conversation was never going to go his way, and stole one last look at the gorgeous 'Madonna' before he took the elevator down to the level of commoners.*

EMILE COMES TO THE END OF HIS LETTER.

In conclusion Emile asked Maria Elena if she was growing tired of reading this. In any case, he said, he was tired of *writing* it. He wished her well, hoped she was in good health. He mentioned that he still had most of his hair, although some was gray. He admitted he was weary but at least his heart was still running like a Model T Ford. He felt he was not emotional in the daylight, at least vocally, but his feelings would explode in the darkened cinema which often immersed him within the benevolence of humanity.

He attached a small picture of his granddaughter and one of himself. Thankfully, Maria Elena saved the letter; unfortunately,

in her. Both struggled on and on in adversity. If there was a difference it had to be devotion to family. There, Emile was, at least on the surface, the complete opposite. But deeper down the similarity was there: no matter how bad things got, both refused to negotiate.

WE HAVE BECOME CONVINCED through this letter that Emile had reached bottom emotionally. The country's economic depression never seemed to have an end, his family was virtually dead to him, and his lover was gone, probably dead, in Spain. He wrote at the end of his long, novel-like letter that it was not a novel because it was unlikely to end well. Was this his final statement on his mental condition he wanted to share with his cousin? Maybe he was not as depressed as he sounded. Maybe he had in the back of his mind the age-old adage of Thomas Fuller, 1650.

"It is always darkest just before the day dawneth."

But we know now that there had to be two. And the most recent one was definitely the Malm's. At some time earlier he shifted families. It was almost certain at the Malm's where he burned almost all his paintings, save for the one that Pier Malm rescued. Go to the Appendix, Figure 3 to peruse the Malm-Loughlin-Jensen family tree.

During the Great Depression it was common for several families to share a home for economy. In the case of the Malm's, four families lived together. For a number of years the Malm's and their extended family lived in Philadelphia or its suburbs. In the 1930s they were in a suburb called, Plymouth Meeting. The family included Axel and Alma, their son Pier, their daughter Edmee, and son-in-law Elliott Loughlin. About that time Alma's nephew Niels Jensen, his wife Lisa and their daughter Bitten joined them. Bitten, who helped in the research for this book, was born in 1929 and told us that she could remember that Emile always lived with them. Assuming her first memories began when she was four, this would put the date at 1933 when the four families that including Emile were living together. Given this new information Emile's *Camino Real* story has to be modified. It is likely that Emile used the Malm-Loughlin-Jensen household as a home base from which he would sally forth in search of work.

When Edmee Loughlin became pregnant with Edmee Kay, the Malm's had to find a larger place. About 1937 they moved from the suburban setting in Plymouth Meeting to one in a rural environment. They found the perfect site … a large, spreading farmhouse near the quaint, little town of North

After college they both found jobs in New York City and were near each other again. Their apartments were on opposite sides of 10th St. in downtown Manhattan on the East Side, and they communicated by yelling across the narrow street from their windows. The time was what the newspapers called the Roaring Twenties.

To give this all some perspective, Frank's mother's diary and autobiography did *not* speak of the frenetic 'roaring anything'. Most of her time was spent living 'small', working as a nurse for the Edison Corporation in Manhattan, a borough of New York City. This meant commuting back and forth to work, doing laundry, shopping and cooking, hanging out with her older sister Dorothea and cousin Priscilla. She and Priscilla occasionally dated guys, but she was yet to meet co-author Frank's dad, Francis James Butterworth Jr., AKA Butts. In other words, for the common man (and woman, and kid), it was not pages from the *Great Gatsby* (F. Scott Fitzgerald's popular novel) or Flappers dancing the Charleston to hot jazz, sipping bootleg gin, or watching the stock market run up to dazzling wealth.

No, exciting headlines were balanced by daily routines. Exciting stories were read but rarely experienced by the working citizen. While my mother toiled in New York, Frank's father-to-be spent his routine life in Philadelphia. He lived at home with his parents while he taught high school English. As a lot of English teachers, he dreamed about writing the Great American Novel (a la Fitzgerald or Hemingway or Clemens). His big adventure was traveling from prosaic Philadelphia with his pals to exciting Manhattan in New

"But in the ten days it took their boat to cross the Atlantic, the money world had changed. Down, down, and away went all those golden profits. Already the French, used to their own postwar depression, were referring in their newspapers to "Le Craque du Wall Street," and they were rather malicious about it."

The main character's friend wrote her at Christmas time, 1929.

"You are going to come back to a changed Etats Unis, and you must let me know your reaction. It is in the air. I notice it like a doe sniffing danger. A curious wildness. A sort of unprincipled disregard of consequence. The stock market affair is one beautiful example. The ugly rearing head of gangsters another. The indecent degree of drinking and flirting, too— prohibition is doomed or else somebody has got to do something about it. But nobody does."

Priscilla Buntin, no different than most people during the Great Depression lost her job, and she moved from New York to Philadelphia to stay with the Butterworth family when they returned from France. She was the first in the family to benefit from Roosevelt's new programs - she was hired as an executive assistant with the Works Progress Administration. The WPA, first funded in 1935, a product of the Depression, was a part of the administration's development plans for creating jobs particularly to rebuild US infrastructure. But the

the country. They had grown with a daughter Kate and her younger brother, co-author Frank. With their family doubled in size the Butterworth's bought a run-down farm near the small town of North Wales where they could really expand - to raise chickens, vegetables, bees, sheep, trees not to mention their kids and anything else that would grow. In the midst of the toil of fixing up the house and the land, the Butterworth's quickly made friends with the neighbors who lived on adjoining farms. One neighbor in particular that they really connected with was the Malm's.

THE MALM'S

Up to this point the probability of Emile becoming Frank's cousin (and this book being written) was still infinitesimally small. But this was about to change.

The Butterworth's got to know the Malm's as a delightfully entertaining, extended family, living in a large farmhouse with a huge adjoining barn on considerable acreage. The family included Axel and Alma Malm, their daughter Edmee, her husband Elliott Loughlin, and their two daughters Edmee Kay and Lynn. Also living there was Alma's nephew Niels Jensen, his wife Lisa and their daughter Bitten. The relationships are detailed in a family tree in Figure 3 in the Appendix. There was a single man there, too… Emile Gauguin.

Frank recalls all of them. He went to school with Edmee Kaye and Lynn. He remembers their mom, Edmee as very good looking like the movie actress Dorothy Lamour. Their father

FRANK'S RECOLLECTIONS OF AXEL, EMILE AND BUTTS

"Outside of the vicious geese and the reeking ram, visits with the Malm's were always fun. Axel Malm was a boisterous, jolly fellow with a big belly, a round, red face, a short-clipped mustache and baldhead, with round, steel-rimmed spectacles. His conversation was explosive and his body, namely his red face and large abdomen, seemed on the verge of exploding. He was always joking exuberantly using loud laughs as punctuation. He had a glass eye and called himself 'Cyclops'. **[Bitten confided with Frank recently that Axel was a "high flier and conned everyone". That was easy to believe.]**

"Emile on the other hand was quiet, somber-looking and rarely smiled or laughed. He was well built and taller than Axel, around 6 feet, 7 inches (2 meters) and at least 200 pounds (90.7 kilos). He always had a serious, almost surprised look, with a gruff demeanor, speaking in guttural, staccato bursts. He was the opposite of buoyantly explosive. But the stern, emotionless exterior intentionally hid his continual wry comments, dramatic story telling, almost always with humorous endings. The actors of that era, Buster Keaton and Fernandel come to mind. Google a 'Fernandel' or 'Buster Keaton' video and you will see Emile in action. A more modern Hollywood version of Emile would be Danny Trejo.

through the minds of these Danish expatriates with their families at risk to the Nazi invaders.

To give a small picture from Wikipedia (http://en.wikipedia. org/wiki/Denm+ark_in_World_War_II) of wartime Denmark, the Nazi occupation of Denmark began April 9, 1940 and continued until the war's end May 5, 1945. Officially 3,000 Danes fled, 4,000 Danish volunteers died fighting on the Eastern Front. Emile's grandson Philippe told us that the Danes were fighting Russians on the Eastern front, meaning that they were fighting as conscripts with the Germans. Philippe noted that his great uncle (Emile's son) Pedro Maria volunteered to fight with the Finns attempting to repulse the Russian invasion. Recent Prime Minister Anders Fogh Rasmussen condemned the 1940-43 Danish government as morally unjustified. Still the Danish Underground caused widespread sabotage, and long labor strikes that forced the Nazis to replace the Danish government with a Nazi military one. And according to the article the Danish government successfully rejected Nazi requests to hand over Jews, disallowed the Danish military to fight for the Nazis, and prevented the Nazi takeover of the Danish courts. It is doubtful that Emile, Axel, and Frank's dad knew any of this at the time. However, it would have been intriguing to have heard Emile's commentary who spent two years in Denmark when Hitler's political rise was reaching a peak.

COLLISION COURSE

As the chapter title implies, rocket ships were involved. Indeed there were two rocket ships that had long before been launched,

On Thursday, September 21, 1939 (11 months after Emile gloomily posted his 30-page letter to his cousin), two rocket ships gently docked. Axel brought Emile over to see Butts' new 1939 Chevrolet. And Pris and Emile were introduced. Katie's diary in her typically terse, emotionless style does not speak of Cupid's arrows. But Priscilla saw this good-looking dude, tall, strong, a rugged handsomeness in his brow, making brilliant conversation particularly in art. Try as she might her feet would not touch the ground.

Emile could not stop showing off, talking in several languages telling anecdotes about bandits in the Colombian Andes or carbon dioxide poisoning in a gold mine in California, or the idiocy of Danish mores. Even *he* thought his stories were more amusing than he normally spun them. Perhaps it was her throaty giggles. He was quickly being smitten.

But Katie does note that during the next couple of weeks there were a flurry of visits, Emile at the Malm's and Priscilla to the Butterworth's with dinners and get-togethers. We simply have to assume that the visit frequency was evidence that Cupid did fire his arrows and Pris and Emile were badly wounded.

Not long later (Sunday, October 21, 1939) exactly 30 days after their initial meeting, Pris and Emile became an 'item'. For the first time in Katie's diary, he 65 and she 43, arrived at the Butterworth house, together. From then on, one read in the diary: "Pris and Emile visit". We would have to assume that this was the courtship period because from time-to-time over the next 5 to 6 months, Pris would occasionally visit alone (perhaps

Emile won big time. After 66 years of heart-breaking losses (e.g. Reconciliation I, II, and III) he won the lotto of love.

HOW THE LOTTO WORKED

There were a large number of improbabilities on how Emile became Frank's cousin-in-law and surrogate grandfather. It took some incredible odds. Here are some of them. It required the duplicity of colleagues that Emile be fired from the Sugamuxi and Tundama Electric Company in Sogamoso, that attempts to reconcile with Olga failed three separate times, that Emile was recruited by Malm Engineering, that his relationship with the Malm's continued, that none of the jobs he had on the *Camino Real* ever became permanent, that he returned to Philadelphia. It took Frank's cousin Priscilla to move to Philadelphia, it took his parents to move next to *and* befriend the Malm's, it took the Malm's to bring Emile over when Pris was there. If you assigned probabilities to all the above steps and multiply them, Pris and Emile won the lotto of love. How about a one in 100 million chance of this happening? And author Frank too won, a real, live grandfather. Not only that, but a grandpa who could ride, shoot, sing and get women … and maybe all at the same time.

Publishing this book, to be a win for Emile's grandchildren, took even greater odds. Besides the above, Pris and Emile had to move to Florida to the same village where co-author David lived who was already a Paul Gauguin fan and who upon discovering Emile's grave, wanted to explore his history; and through extensive detective work located a surviving person

radio. We had air-raid drills, darkened our window at night with pieces of particle board called Masonite, Dad cut to fit exactly. They were stored near the windows during the day, ready to be pushed into place at dusk. And I became particularly adept at memorizing silhouettes of German, Japanese and US warplanes so that we could 'call in' our sighting of any suspicious aircraft. We would rush outdoors with binoculars when we heard the roar of planes overhead. But the air-raid warden program and drills began in 1942. So, my memory went back at least that far. Fortunately we were never bombed in the US."

But Emile's granddaughter, Mette Gauguin, wrote to us that her older sister was not so lucky. She was killed by a bomb during an air raid by the Brits (see Mette's emails in the Appendix). And a similar thing happened to one of Frank's German colleagues who was grossly disfigured by an American bomb.

"WWII permeated our lives even on vacation. As a young boy I recall walking along the Atlantic beach in New Jersey and was warned by my mother not to step in the black sticky globs in the sand. These I learned later were congealed oil from Nazi U-Boat-launched torpedoes that sunk our tankers and merchant ships possibly killing their crews. Petroleum congeals into globs of tar when it reacts with seawater. These globs

Emile first came on the scene, I was taken to see the recently released (1939) movie, *The Wizard of Oz*. I recall the movie vividly with its screaming witches and flying monkeys. I was one terrified, four-year-old dude. All this puts my distinct memories back to 1939, the time when Emile Gauguin entered the scene. So although I don't specifically recall the first meeting of Pris and Emile, I must have been aware of them. And although my memories of Pris and Emile grew more intense as I became older, I had to have remembered them in those early years."

1940 to 1950. These visits were rich experiences for all of us. They generally involved intense conversations over teas and meals. All that remains are the following anecdotes. Throughout this book at appropriate places Frank has inserted Emile's stories that had over time became 'Emilian' legends. The following are a few more incidents involving Priscilla and Emile and the Butterworth's. They are indented and in quotes to indicate Frank is telling them.

HE IS JUST A LITTLE BOY

"Once, in the early 1940s Pris and Emile went with us to a local restaurant in nearby North Wales. It was an adventure to go to a restaurant then, a special occasion during the war, particularly with Pris and Emile and the four of us. I loved the deviled crab there. Once during dinner I had to go to the bathroom. My mother decided to take me, I was about five then, with her to the ladies room and made the mistake of asking the waiter for permission. The waiter hesitated for a minute, forcing my mother to add, "He is just a little boy." My mother meant that I was too little to go on my own. But Emile deliberately misinterpreted it to mean that my mother was assuring the waiter there would be nothing improper or kinky. I didn't understand the off-color nature at the time, and still don't for a different reason. I don't know how my mother felt inside, but

eye. He awoke with a jolt, jumped up and chased me around the yard yelling, unintelligibly at me. He never caught me, but I felt so bad for playing the trick. And he did, too, when he started to realize he was the butt of a joke and how scared and embarrassed I felt. In any event, it never affected our friendship. I was always his favorite. But I was always a little more careful with pranks. And he was a bit more careful and slept, as he did as a war fighter, with one eye open. [**Check out the picture of me and my bicycle directly in front of the place where Emile was snoozing.**]"

EMILE GETS RELIGION, SORT OF

"Shortly after the war, my family and I toured the US for a year. We towed an old camper trailer, a Gilkie made 20 years earlier in Terre Haut Illinois. It had two slide-out double beds and canvas sides and top. My Uncle Donald Macomber took his eight-member family on a two-month, camping-adventure trip out west with it in 1929. My father and I refurbished it: replacing the wooden-spoked wheels and narrow tires with modern wheels and tires, a tow bar, towing lights etc. This modified trailer was incredibly rugged, serving the Macomber family for many years afterward. For a good part of the time we lived in that trailer [**Franks hopes to soon publish this**

which, again lo and behold, had the correct Chevy axle. The mechanic duly noted that we had a guardian angel. Because of the war shortages it might have been weeks before we could have proceeded. I do not know if Emile heard that story; but if he had, he might have been more assured of his theological conclusion. Knowing what I already know now about Emile, he probably could have fixed it himself.

But when I at the age of 13 heard Emile's interest in our 1946-7 trip, I kind of wrote him off as a city slicker, green horn never having experienced the rigors that we did. Little did I know now what he went through in Colombia or on the *Camino Real*.

THE GIFT RADIO

"When I was a young teenager, most likely soon after we returned from our trip around the US in 1947, Pris and Emile gave me a radio. Then, it was a big deal to have your own radio…an erstwhile iPod. It was not just a radio, but one that Emile made for me from bits and pieces of electronic gear. The most memorable part of it was the case that covered the transformer and vacuum tubes etc. (long before transistors). It was a rectangular box, about 5X5X7 inches (13X13X18 centimeters) he made out of hard cardboard (or very thin wood) that he covered with a collage of pictures he thought I might like in color cut from magazines glued on the top and

exciting experience. The entire group was involved giving even the kids a role. So we all had ownership.

"My sister in one performance at the age of 14 was asked to wear an embarrassing costume or should I say no costume. Emile wanted the other team to guess one of his father's paintings of a group of bare-chested Tahitian women. Emile unthinkingly suggested that that Kate and Priscilla 'dress' (or actually undress) as Tahitian women, my sister Kate, a shy and young teenager, absolutely refused. Emile realized his blunder and honored her request without another word or sense of shame. But aside from that, for us kids, this was a wonderful opportunity to be part of the adult world give or take a few points because in this case, a little too adult. But Kate saw it as a triumph in her assertiveness, winning an argument with adults. She saved the day for her mom and Pris." **[Looking back on it, we could say Emile was being an asshole. Obviously, the women would not have gone along with it.]**

THE GUITARS: SONGS AND CHORDS

"While the Malm's were homesick for Denmark, I think that Emile was homesick for Colombia because around 1948 in his Ardmore house he showed me a Colombian-style guitar he had made, and then, when Priscilla wanted to play, he made her a smaller one.

What was also impressive, Frank recalls, is that Emile remembered these songs and that he taught Pris to sing them in Spanish, too. Now, many years later, he was even more impressed. Frank wrote, "Knowing only rudimentary Spanish, learning songs in that language is no small feat. I am OK with Feliciano's *Feliz Navidad* but I still struggle with the mariachi ballad, *Amorcito Corazon*". We are guessing now that Emile had someone instructing him, maybe a *Colombiana linda* (a pretty Colombian girl). Perhaps he learned to sing them around the evening campfire after work building roads. One purpose was to find a sure way to a senorita's heart. This is a probable reason because having a large repertoire of songs is a requirement for Latinos.

When co-author Frank was about 13, he related, "Emile taught me how to play a few chords and rhythmic strumming for Colombian songs on my ukulele. It is possible that Pris and Emile gave me the ukulele. Later, I played the chords and strumming on my guitar. It didn't matter to me that these were chords were not in any North American chord books. They gave an unusual, impressive sound listeners at a parties in graduate school I thought they would enjoy. Then, if that did not work, I would give them the spiel that I learned them from Paul Gauguin's son."

The name of the instrument baffled Bitten and Frank. He recalled seeing the instruments and hearing them played in the Ardmore house. Bitten also recalled Emile playing the instrument earlier in North Wales that may have been a three-stringed instrument, but could not remember the name. Frank thought Priscilla called it a 'tipple' close to the name (tica or teka) that Florence Johnson thought Emile told her.

often, we were told, but no letters have been found. Blanca was seven when Emile left Colombia and passed away in 1999.

THEY MOVED AWAY

In 1950 at ages 76 and 54, respectively, Emile and Priscilla, decided to move from the Philadelphia area in Pennsylvania to Englewood a small town on the West Coast of Florida on the Gulf of Mexico. As you might have already guessed, Emile's moves required a safe place to land. And it was into the arms of another Danish connection: Elsa Jensen, Alma Malm's niece.

Elsa was originally from Denmark, moved from Philadelphia to Chicago and married a wealthy real estate developer, John "Jack" Foster Bass. He had so much money he followed his ultimate life plan to create a World-class, marine biological, research station there, called Bass Biological Laboratory and Zoological Research Supply Company.

With the deaths of Alma and Axel Malm, Elsa urged Pris and Emile to move to Englewood to stay near her in one of the cottages on the Bass Labs campus for $50 per month. Compared to Ardmore with higher rents and snowy, slushy winters, this was paradise. Pris wrote glowing letters to her cousin Katie, re-counting visions of a perpetual summer of flowers and bloom-ing shrubs and sailing, being right on the waters of the Gulf of Mexico just a few steps from their back door. All Pris had to do was go out her back door and jump into her boat and she was off sailing. Frank's mother, also an avid sailor, was tempted to move there, but too many restrictions were involved such

sawed in rounds. They kind of looked like cookies sliced from a roll of cookie dough, stood on their edges and mortared together. Architecturally speaking, the "cookie house" style is truly unique. Florida State's Division of Historic Resources says they are unaware of any other such structures in the whole state, or the whole country for that matter. The institute invited distinguished biologists from around the World to stay in the small, cookie houses for a year or two to carry out their research in the laboratory and obtain specimens from the nearby Gulf.

THE SAILBOAT

Always the craftsman and engineer Emile satisfied Priscilla's love of sailing, by designing and building her a small sailboat again demonstrating his incredible abilities to design and carry out the construction. Looking at the photos, it is hard to identify a specific class of sailboat, so we can assume it was another Emile original, he called it the *Noa Noa,* named after his dad's Tahitian journal, a multimedia, highly spiritual memoir. We dwell on this building project partly because of Emile's craftsmanship, but because it reveals a little something about his love for Pris, an inveterate sailor. From the looks of it, it seems to be kind of clunky and slow. Throughout their Florida years Pris would write Katie with snapshots and accounts the Butterworth's loved to get. Some of the snapshots were of the *Noa Noa.* See Photographs III by Pris documenting the building and sailing of the boat. Note the house where they lived can be seen in the background from the workshop.

two such encounters according to co-author, David, that were recorded in the local newspapers. One person inquired whether he owned any of his father's "originals", to which EG responded "You are looking at one"! The other encounter was less complimentary, when in a retail shop, the salesclerk recognized the name on his bank check and commented "That's a very famous name. Wasn't he a famous French painter who ran away to Tahiti to paint and died of gonorrhea?" Whereupon, a 'puffed up' Emile responded, "My father died of syphilis!" Then, he squared his shoulders, with head held aloof, and exited the store.

In an email Diana Harris wrote us, "I met Priscilla about 1964 when I bought a small vacation cottage two blocks from her famous "cookie house" where she was living. We had a good deal in common because we both had such unique houses...mine being built totally of ship wrecks from the 1916 hurricane. She was very fond of children and on occasion, would walk to my house to bring a book to share with my children. She was a fabric designer and weaver with a large loom sitting in the "cookie house". Diana's friend Leah Lasbury still has chairs upholstered in fabric Priscilla wove.

"There was one incident which always brings a smile to my face," wrote Diana, "when I think back on it. I was invited for cocktails to the "cookie house". It was winter, and cool and breezy for Florida. When Priscilla opened the door to her home, she was smiling and laughing. She said I must come in quickly as I could, along with her other guests, enjoy the fact that her house was 'singing'. Over the years, bits of the mortar between the pine-log slices that made up the walls of the cookie

with his enmity about government welfare. Priscilla had a Social Security number, but was unable to collect a monthly check until 1961. Pris and Emile never owned a house, and all indications are that they always lived on a low income and probably less in their retirement upon moving to Florida.

Diana Harris wrote that, after Emile's death Priscilla continued to stay in Englewood. She took a job in Leah Lasbury's real estate office as a secretary where she worked until she died.

On November 12, 1966 Priscilla Buntin Gauguin, died in Sarasota Memorial Hospital at age 70. She was cremated and her ashes were buried at the foot of Emile's grave. Priscilla's three-page will is dated January 22, 1965 and names John F. Bass III as executor (the person assigned to carry out her wishes). In paragraph #2, she gave the small pencil sketch by Paul Gauguin to Mette along with a diamond and turquoise ring. Emile's granddaughter, Mette Gauguin wrote co-author David, "I can tell that it was a woman (I may be mistaken) who delivered the Gauguin drawing to my father, Emile (II) in Copenhagen as he was going to visit me in Portugal. I remember that my sister, Aline, met Mother Ellen (Alma's sister, see Figure 3 in the Appendix) when she was in Denmark many years ago. They had corresponded several years before their meeting."

Priscilla's death, 11 years after Emile's, upset Frank's mother terribly. From a family of nonagenarians, 70 was just too young. To her it was unnaturally premature. She was stunned, Frank recalled, in a state of deep mourning for months, they were that close. Perhaps Pris missed Emile so much she died of

Family relationships

His mother was obviously a central figure for Emile. Outside of virtually abandoning him for four years during his elementary schooling, we would have to say he had a deep love for her. He appeared to have resisted her controlling influence when he was a young man, then acquiesced giving her a stronger role in developing his family life: he did give her a daughter-in-law and grandchildren. But he ultimately refused to return home to her and he denied her influence up to her death. Although it might not appear important to most of us, there were issues such as his teasing her for her educational inadequacies had had a negative impact on them both when he reflected back.

The time spent with his father was understandably far shorter, but his influence might have been much greater, a haunting specter. The first six years of Emile's life, we surmise, must have been good ones being number one son and Paul, then, being more of a family man. But the absences began early. When Paul did visit Denmark, the family times were no longer than a year. Although we concluded that he probably had the best associations with Emile because Emile's French must have been better than his siblings. But then again, Emile was probably away at school. Still Emile was always in awe of his father, and throughout his life continually felt inadequate and second rate. There appeared to be little love between each other.

He gave his brothers, Jean and Pola, a mixture of grudging praise, jealousy and disapproval slightly favoring Jean. But there was definite animosity among the three. We would have this long-term bitterness, and Emile may have found a sympathetic comrade. She may have assured Emile that his father was not the icon he had built in his mind - that it was all right to show some disrespect.

The relationship Emile had with his cousin and father's niece, Maria Elena, seemed to us to have by 1938 the most maturity and respect. The evidence for this is strong and direct. He had known her over a span of many years: once as children in Paris, again for a few years when she was raising her family in Bogota, and then, by letter writing. Our guess is that he may have held her the closest of all the others because there were fewer conflicts. By the tone of his letter it was likely he now gave her ultimate respect due to her aura. She was an awesome personage: brilliant, a mother of 10, very wealthy, and firmly established in her society. When Emile, at the most vulnerable time of his life, learned in a roundabout way that Maria Elena wanted to resume contact with him, it set off an eruption of memories which resulted in his 1938 letter.

The history of the 1938 letter was amusing by its formality. Maria Elena wanted to get back in contact with Emile after perhaps 20 years and wrote to a friend in common, Mrs. Genevieve Levison, in Copenhagen for Emile's address. Genevieve did not know it and wrote to Emile's old Parisian friend, Wiehe (the one who found Emile the cab-driver job). He then wrote to Emile to get his permission to send it to Maria Elena – Emile explained to Maria Elena that this was common among Danes. In the process Emile learned from Mrs. Levison that Maria Elena held a certain fondness for him and that their friendship went back many years.

toto it lasted at least 25 years which passes the time criterion, but none were intimate as a family. Bitten and Kate could have been his virtual granddaughters, and Frank, his virtual grandson. None of us could recall an angry incident. And the relationships were on a take it or leave it nature with little commitment required. And when Priscilla arrived, she likely mollified any awkward scenes

The ultimate personal relationship was with Priscilla for 16 uninterrupted years of contented bliss. All that he desired in a relationship was with Priscilla. His needs for love and companionship were met. Of course his 10-year relationship with his virtual grandson, co-author Frank, was excellent, too. It is possible that any feeling of disrespect for Frank, were quickly but gently smothered by Priscilla. Recall the maple-seed incident. Also recall that Priscilla spent time by letters befriending his Danish family. So it seems that his relationship-forming ability improved over the years, perhaps through practice. Certainly Priscilla's influence gently diffused his negative attitude toward others. In a sense, Priscilla broke this bronco and he did not resist her transformative influence.

GRANDFATHERLY ABILITY

Throughout the narrative co-author Frank has called Emile his virtual grandfather. And one of the reasons for this book was to describe him to his real, estranged grandchildren who might well ask, how was he as a grandfather? The answer: pretty good. Many of the above recollections of Frank's exemplify

is so important with having a steady job, particularly if you don't need a steady income with few commitments.

Although Emile lists jobs he had, he does not say much about why the jobs had such a short duration. He just wrote 'the job ended'. The two longest jobs lasted six years each and could have been longer if the companies had not failed. For the *Camino Real* jobs, they ran out of work or money to pay wages. In the case of his position as a combatant, the war ended. According to Archila he was fired in three of them. Outside of the one that ended for economic reasons, we are tempted to conclude that he was fired from all the others. Emile carefully did not tell Maria Elena about those latter jobs and perhaps he was silent about how he lost the others. No one, we are sure, can be proud of screw-ups.

EMILE'S SELF-PERCEPTION

What he wrote about himself was often self-deprecating. He wanted others to know that he could never hope to achieve what his father did and felt that others might wonder why he was such a failure. He, in the same breath, said that the name 'Gauguin' was a curse. But we can be sure that it opened a lot of doors. Perhaps this gave him the confidence to be able to get another position. Curse or no curse he had a famous name.

But to himself, he knew he was pretty awesome. The book details his long, dazzling list of abilities. True, he could not hold a job, and rather than look inside himself, or struggle to overcome whatever it was that kept from staying with the same

and do accounting. Who cares about a nest egg or a net worth with those qualifications? Nest eggs, he may have countered, were for people who lacked confidence.

Bottom line: We have spent a lot of words failing him on personal relationships and his spotty career, but this would have been a boring book to research, write or read if he had been anyone else.

His Legacy

We have listed and described what we learned. Perhaps wives and children would have added a lot more. Perhaps his grandchildren and great grandchildren might add to the story. He may have not achieved his goals, and we will probably never know. But he always seemed in retrospect to be happy through the mountains and valleys of his life, he was ready with a continuous flow of funny stories with what he had, but unhappy with what he refused to acknowledge – his Danish family.

According to his grandson Philippe living in Copenhagen who never met him, Emile has left a huge physical legacy of descendants. There are at least forty-seven sets of genes with the Danish side: 8 grand-, 15 great-grand- and 21 great-great-grand-children from his marriage with Olga and possibly, but improbably, a few sets of genes in Colombia. Despite our attempts to inquire with Gauguin heirs in Colombia and the US, very few memories survived there. But we do know that the Gauguin genes are present in at least 93 living heirs from his Aunt Marie Gauguin de Uribe.

about Emile Gauguin". The answer was, "A lot. He was my virtual grandfather". And there began a long and productive friendship and the start of this book.

David brought Frank up to date on how he envisioned the project, and from then on, they worked together. David continued with a tremendous amount of tedious work researching, checking and sharing with Frank vital records including birth certificates, immigration documents, ship manifests, wills, and death certificates. He did not have much to go on, but bit-by-bit he pieced together a profile of Emile Gauguin. He wrote this up first as an outline (see Time Line in the Appendix) and then, as an eight-page biography. He also appended reminiscences by Diana Harris a writer and reporter from Englewood who also recovered news articles and other useful background.

In the meantime, Frank began working on his recollections of Emile. He wrote: "Over an 11-year period as I grew from childhood to a teenager about to enter high school, Emile became my close 'buddy'". These memories took the form of anecdotes, many scattered in various chapters, but most ended up in the section labeled the US Years.

Conversations through email and phone they kept each other up to date on their findings which led to questions and discussions on how to obtain further leads, how to interpret perceived incongruities and puzzling gaps.

At the same time David was able to make contact with a number of European Gauguins: Mette, Jacques and Philippe Gauguin (Emile's grandchildren), Michala and Jonas Gauguin (Jacques' children) and Clovis Gauguin (the grandson of Emile's

a first-blush review. Comments came back ranged from 'disorganized junk' to 'fantastic'. Both humbled and elated we pressed on, we knew it was disorganized by its very nature, but it was *not* junk. We knew we had a gold mine. And the '*fantastics*' egged us on.

The big challenge was filling huge gaps in his life that were unaccounted for, namely the 17 years in Colombia and the 22 years he lived in the US before he met Frank. The only definite information beside what we had already collected just gave us inklings. We began to make educated guesses about his family, his wedding and his children, one of his jobs, and an anecdote of two, steamship sailings, etc. But as it turned out, these guesses were colossally and embarrassingly wrong.

Frank began to investigate the gaps by searching for genealogical links to Paul Gauguin's sister Marie Gauguin de Uribe. After a while he was able to get a name or two. One genealogist, Francisco Carbone had on his web page, what turned out to be a fairly large Uribe-Gauguin family tree. Fantastic as it was we still wanted to converse with a few of them. Trying to keep the Uribe's privacy intact Senor Carbone indirectly put Frank in contact with another genealogist, Jesus Chacon, who knew Emile's distant cousins, the Uribe's. He sent emails out to them. But nothing happened. Complete silence. We were about to give up, when he gave Frank an email address to one of the relatives. This time we sent out a plea for contact telling this person about our project, that one of us is a long distant cousin ("Ok! Ok!"... cousin-in-law), and how we longed to converse with someone about their interesting Danish cousin.

Elena Uribe, summarizing his life in the US. It was almost as if Emile anticipated the needs for more details to his biographers, and we are grateful that the Uribe family saved this letter for 77 years. And what a letter it was! Information in it nearly filled the rest of the gaps. It covered key events that occurred during the 17 years he lived in Colombia and the two decades Emile lived in the US. After we transcribed, translated and interpreted it, we realized that many of our suppositions about Emile and his earlier life had to be revised, reinterpreted and rewritten. We learned more about his employment, we could follow step-by-step in exciting detail of his attempts to keep his family together. We were treated to his dramatic accounts to fight off the effects of the Great Depression. Plus he provided accounts of his father's death and stories about his mother, brothers and his children. Patience pays!

At the outset before this flood of data, we had found a Wikipedia article in Spanish about Emile, but some of the material was so egregiously wrong we wondered about the veracity of the rest. However, with the new materials we were better able to judge its credibility over all, and we were confident to move toward completion. And as we combined the massive information from the Uribe-Gauguin family a clearer picture began to take shape. We were finished with the data collection. We were ready begin to write and eventually to finally consider going to press.

The 1938 letter was a jewel. It was so fresh and poignant, in a way, it outshone the rest of the book, an autobiography

Edgar Alzate for their poignant recollections. Gratitude goes to Professor Tilar Mazzeo for helping Frank use various techniques for creative nonfiction. Thanks go to Jonas Gauguin, the Valencia Writers' Group, Manuela Hargassner-Delpos and Sara Schneider for their helpful feedback on Chapter 1. Appreciation is extended to Frank's wife, Patricia Butterworth, and daughter, Lisa Butterworth, for help with translations, to Frank's sister-in-law, Cristina Ramirez, for transcriptions and his niece, Diana Ramirez, for scanning, sizing and editing photos. Thanks go to Annette Buhl Sorensen for locating Emile's academic records at the Polytecknist Laereantalt. Thanks also go to our wives Lois and Patricia for help throughout the process and for their patience and encouragement during the whole ordeal. Appreciation and accolades go to Elizabeth Williamson, Professor of English, who graciously and tirelessly line-edited this book. There are many more people to thank but the number is too numerous to list here.

<u>Warning</u>: We have tried to get multiple sources to support statements, claims and conclusions and have often made reference to them with links. One of the most frequently used sources was Wikipedia because it was one of the first links that appeared in a search and that it looked complete. Still we include here Wikipedia's own disclaimer that says that it does not have ultimate control over the editing, leaving it up to a honest, informed and interested group of volunteer editors. http://en.wikipedia.org/wiki/Wikipedia:General_disclaimer.

1. GAUGUIN GENES AT WORK

[In writing this book about the life of Emile Gauguin, we came upon some relatives of note. Some have been covered in the narrative, and four others here in detail: a celebrated engineer (Pedro) and three painters of note (Clovis, Santiago, and Mette). Apologies to all of you talented and deserving Gauguin-Uribe heirs we missed. Let us know for a next edition.]

A. PEDRO URIBE GAUGUIN

CURRICULUM VITAE

[The curriculum vitae (CV) of Pedro Uribe, Emile's first cousin, was provided by and published by the Uribe family, translated from the Spanish by Patricia Butterworth and edited for style by the authors whose comments are in square brackets.]

He was born in Paris on December 17, 1879. Son of Juan Uribe Buenaventura and Marie Gauguin, the only sister of the painter Paul Gauguin.

Doctor Uribe Gauguin made his first studies in Paris and arrived to Colombia when he was 14 years old (1893); he studied for a year in a Jesuit's school to learn Spanish and then he went to Switzerland to study engineering at the University of Lausanne when after 10 years he graduated in June 14 1904. He traveled to United States and Mexico arriving back to his

From 1905 through 1953, he was part of the faculty of the School of Mathematics and Engineering in the National University and was its dean from 1923-1925.

He worked also as a chief engineer in the railroad of Ibague-Armenia, this construction was sponsored by a French company, but unfortunately it was suspended. He was called by Dr. Carlos E. Restrepo to be in charge of the Occident branch, but he rejected the offer due to his health.

From 1929-1946 he was the president of the National Council of Railroads and had a notable participation in Bocas de Ceniza project.

In 1939 he was appointed as president of the Colombian Delegation to the III Congress of Roads in Santiago, Chile, where he was decorated and appointed as a member of the Engineering Institute of Chile.

President, Dr. Alfonso Lopez Pumarejo gave him the decoration of the Order of Boyaca [**This is Colombia's highest peacetime honor by the then President of Colombia.**] President Dr. Laureano Gomez Castro wanted him to preside over the Delegation to a congress in Mexico, but he declined because his age.

After his retirement from the Department of Public Works, he continued serving his country in other activities, because he was dedicated to work in his hacienda in Boluga en Venadillo (Tolima) where he increased the rice production and the improvement of cattle.

At his death he was honorary professor of the National University; honorary member of the Colombian Engineering

PEDRO URIBE GAUGUIN'S TRAVELOGUE:

Voyage from Paris to Bogota [Pedro described his return home from his engineering studies at the University of Lausanne. See Table II in Chapter 3 for ocean travel times, sail or steam.]

November 19th, 1904 left Paris at 4 o'clock from the Gare du Nord by the express Paris to Bolognes **[likely now called Boulogne-sur-Mer due north of Paris on the English Channel]** traveling 256 km in 2.49 hours. Left from Bologna at 10:00 PM on a packet boat which was supposed to take us to a ship which was waiting for us out in the channel. At 11:00 PM we left for America. The boat on which we were traveling, the *Statendam,* is a magnificent structure of more than 10,000 tons. I'd say it's about 140 meters long and 16.5 meters wide. It has three bridges. My cabin is on the first deck underneath the second bridge. As there were very few passengers in first class (43) I am alone in my cabin. My first impression of the boat is very good and I am not mistaken because for the entire trip I had nothing but excellent service and proper from friendly personnel. Even though it's a Dutch ship the food is French, the menus are very well composed and the chef is pretty good. Breakfast is an English breakfast. Three concerts per day. The passengers, most of whom are from North America, are very nice and are very good society. The crossing lasted for nine days and a half; we arrived in New York 29 November at noon. This sea is pretty bad during the entire crossing. The day after our departure we had a storm and the day before our arrival in New York was the worst day with a snowstorm. We had a bit of fog; what made the

I had only two days to visit New York but I threw myself into it without losing a single minute. I walked all of the city in all senses of the word by tram, elevated and subway. I visited the good and the bad areas; I crossed both bridges. What struck me the most was that admirable manner in which transportation was established: very quickly, without interruption and comfortable.

Very little beautiful, very much ugly, a lot of architecture wishing to be new and luxurious but which is mostly just extravagant. In sum, very practical and of poor taste. As I love and admire Paris in comparing it to New York. Paris will have no equal.

Details: The building of 23 stories has about 10 elevators among which some that stop in each floor and others which are express for certain floors only. The subway has four lines: two for the local trains and two for the express. The construction engineers here had more facility than those in Paris; but in Paris the engineers did something beautiful; here only utility, and the elevated of New York should be better run than the viaducts of Metropolitan Paris. I did not see any people with canes. The streets are narrow and poorly maintained.

December 1. At noon I left New York on the boat called *Havana* of the Ward Line, an American company. The boat is 4000 tons approximately; the first-class cabins are good and situated on the bridge deck; but the service is bad, dirty and we ate poorly; there is a lack of largess and comfort. I can compare this boat with that of the Dutch company which brought me from Europe and my impression is quite poor for this one.

December 12. Departure for Salina Cruz at seven AM. A single man carried my two trunks weighing 83 kg from the city to the train station about 4 km away.

We arrived around noon in Tierra Blanca where we had to change trains. The train that was supposed to take us at noon didn't arrive until midnight. We slowly continued our voyage on a really bad track which made one ask how we were even able to traverse it. Around 2 o'clock in the afternoon we were stopped by a train derailment in front of us; at 6 PM, the track finally clear, we could continue. Around 9 o'clock we stopped in a village where we passed the night.

We were forced to sleep on the banquettes in the train car because there was no place to sleep in the village.

December 14. At 7 AM we left. 9 km before Santa Lucrecia, we derailed; as we were going at 4 miles an hour we didn't even realize that our train had derailed. The rail employees, used to such an event, quickly got us back on the rails and we continued; 2 km further on another derailment.

At noon we finally arrived at Santa Lucrecia where we had to change trains.

We took the train for Tehuantepec at 8 PM and arrived in Tehuantepec 24 hours late taking 60 hours to cover about 500 km.

December 15. I left for Salina Cruz. The encampment where I was supposed to go is one hour from the village. I arrived there around 10 o'clock at night.

December 16. After several days I decided to leave for Bogota. Thanks to Celiane Dessan, who proved herself to be

January 18. Left Panama at 8 AM. Arrived in Colon at 10 AM. In Panama I stayed at the Marina Hotel run by a Frenchman, very correct. A first-class ticket on the railroad from Panama to Colon was $5 [**perhaps pesos**]; for the luggage three cents per English pound. The transport of my two trunks cost me $5.70 at least 12 times more than in France. In Colon I stayed at Astor house. We ate well.

Panama is very ugly; the part built by the French; in Ancon is charming and clean. Colon is better than Panama; cleaner. The American influence is at least 90 percent of the other influences. I was taken by a great sadness upon seeing this magnificent work escape the French.

January 23. Left: at 6 PM on the French packet boat, *Saint-Germain* of the Generale Translantique company. The ship was stranded the whole night.

January 24. The ship left at 3 AM. Agitated ocean.

January 25. Arrived in Puerto Colombia at 9 AM. Arrived in Baranquilla at 11 AM.

January 26. Left Baranquilla on the boat *Isabel*. Small but agreeable. Ever since Magangue we are only seven passengers; from Gamarra we were just five. The river is very dry; despite this we had a good trip. We passed several boats; none of them caught up with us. Five hours from Varada a tree branch made a 6 cm x 20 cm hole in the boat which we repaired within an hour. Some damage to the motor was also quickly repaired. These difficulties caused us to lose about two days. We arrived in La Dorada in 12 days.

February 7. Arrived in La Dorada and in Honda.

line 3 in 1904 any of which Pedro might have ridden on. Some of the best examples of Art Nouveau decorations were placed there by the designers of the subways, although they did not know what to call it at the time. The cosmetic differences between the subways in the two cities continue to this today.

After Pedro departed Havana sailing south to Mexico on the Yucatan Peninsula (Merida), the itinerary became complicated. After Merida they steamed northward to Veracruz, Mexico, where he took a cross-country train southward to the Pacific beach community of San Benito, now a surfer's paradise in the State of Oaxaca. Although it seemed a beautiful vacation side trip in itself, he visited with (we have to speculate) a family friend Celiane Dessan. After that he sailed southward along the Guatemalan coast making many stops until he arrived at the City of Panama in a recently-formed country, formerly part of Colombia. Taking a short train ride across the Isthmus to Colon he departed by ship to Barranquilla, Colombia, for his final, arduous overland leg of his homeward trip to Bogota.

The Panama Railway Company was built almost 50 years earlier to accommodate the California Gold Rush and later during the canal construction, transported the dead bodies to hospitals and medical schools who paid handsomely for the thousands of laborers who died tragically during construction (Wikipedia.com).

Pedro's "great sadness upon seeing this magnificent work" when he entered Colon most likely referred to the

PEDRO URIBE'S LETTER TO HIS
SISTER MARIA ELENA

[**Our commentary: Pedro Uribe Gauguin's letter (translated by Patricia Butterworth) to his sister Maria Elena requested a fair distribution of their mother's belongings following her death in 1918 gives the reader a rare glimpse into the lives of Paul Gauguin's niece and nephew. Some of these items, if not all, had sentimental value to them because it is likely they were brought here by Maria Gauguin de Uribe from Paris. Recall Manuel Roca's commentary about Maria Gauguin de Uribe's ordeal transporting these items from Puerto Colombia to Bogota.**]

Dear Elena,

Distribution that can take place, in my understanding, of some of the things that my mother left to us and the list that Miguel had required for the same purpose.

	To me	To Elena
1.	Furniture and little frames and some items I have in my living room.	My mother's jewelry
2.	A tea pot, coffee maker and silver tray	Two silver trays, silverware and some things to use on the table: (sugar container, salad bowl, etc.)
3.	Carmen's photograph (#) Carmen's little cup (goblet) (#)	The two paintings, portraits of my grandmothers.
4.	A box containing little spoons for coffee and ice cream, made of vermeil with monogram (#). The ring I gave in my mother's name as a present on my wedding day.	The small tapestry The pouf from the living room. A bronze column

of Emile's cousins in their houses and what they felt is valuable including Pedro's poignant request for the portrait and tiny cup of his twin sister Carmen who died very young and was buried in Paris. We assumed that Maria Elena and Miguel lived separate from her mother, but the distribution of property was not yet completed two years after she died suggested by the remark that some of the objects were in Miguel's (Maria Elena's husband) house. From the Roca article discussed below in the Appendix, we can conclude it was likely that much of the belongings were transported from Paris.

The mention of two portraits of his grandmothers made us wonder which grandmother's: Aline or one of Juan N.'s mother and whether they were portraits of his grandmother by Paul Gauguin who was not very famous then and did not bear mentioning. In the Colombia narrative and Photographs sections the possibility of Gauguin canvasses has been discussed.

The Arosa frame likely refers to the wealthy art collector and conservator for Marie Gauguin, Gustave Arosa, which seemed more important to them than the painting it held.

Vermiel is silver coated with at least ten-carat gold.

A pouf and a spider could be referring to furniture, an ottoman and table, respectively

Ambelema is a municipality in the Department of Tolima where Pedro had his residence. We know from his CV above that he retired at his hacienda in the same area

B. CLOVIS GAUGUIN (1949-2015)

BIOGRAPHICAL SKETCH AND WORKS

Clovis Gauguin (born 1949 and died 2015, Copenhagen, Denmark) gave up his chance to go to law school to be formerly trained by the celebrated silversmith, Georg Jensen, won a medal for his work in 1969. Self-taught painter and jazz musician.

Exhibitions:
Arles, France 1992
Toulouse, France 1995
Geneva, Switzerland 2002
Grand Chateau, Luxembourg 2005
Kassu Halonen, Finland 2006
Galleri Geo-Art, Denmark 2009 – 2011, 2013

By exploring the concept of landscape in a nostalgic way, Clovis Gauguin investigates the dynamics of landscape, including the manipulation of its effects and the limits of spectacle based on our assumptions of what landscape means to us. Rather than presenting a factual reality, an illusion is fabricated to conjure the realms of our imagination.

His paintings appear as dreamlike images in which fiction and reality meet, well-known tropes merge, meanings shift, past and present fuse. Time and memory always play a key role. By merging several seemingly incompatible worlds into a new universe, he wants to amplify the astonishment of the spectator by creating compositions or settings that generate tranquil

ODE TO PAUL GAUGUIN

[Great-grandson Clovis Gauguin's poem read by him at the 150th anniversary of Paul Gauguin's birth. The occasion was the gathering of the Gauguin clan (65 members from Denmark, Norway and the UK) at Paul Gauguin's grave on Hiva Oa in Autona the Marquesas island to celebrate the 150 years of his birth - 7 June 1998.]

Here you lie buried in the soil, under the sun and the stars
Of the southern sky with the view of the landscape you painted,
And so far away from where your journey started.
Your mind and your hands brought you here on your way seeking the innocent world. Your soul was a burning flame, the colors your guiding stars through the storms of your life
Your palette was the shield against the scornful laughter
When the world woke up to realize that the art
Of painting has changed totally.
The seeds you've planted, have now grown up
And you have become a myth to the World
Still living and breathing through your pictures
In the halls of the famous, next to your friends
Who suffered and fought the same struggles
And paid the price for seeking and opening new doors and
Giving new eyes to see the World.
I might be a stranger right here, but I'm
One of the seeds you planted long ago and
Far from here, today returning with your family
To pay our respect to you, in the place where your eyes

Clovis Henri Gauguin great-grandson of Paul Gauguin
accepting a painting by co-author David in 2004.

1998.   Ancient Artifacts. Santander gallery. Miami

1998.   Lost Fragments of Pompeii. Galeria Americas Collection, Miami, Florida.

1999.   Centro Cultural Pelican Bay. Naples, Florida

2002   Arte Consultores, Bogota, Colombia

2003   Exposicion lanzamiento del libro "Tras las Huellas del tiempo". Embajada de Francia, Bogota, Colombia.

2004   Galeria Julietta Alvarez, Medellin, Colombia.

2005   Galeria Arte Consultores, "Oleos", Bogota

2006   Fundacion Santillana, "Oleos", Bogota.

2008   Arte consultores Bogota

2009   Arte Consultores

2010   Arte Consultores

2011   Museo de Artes Visuales, Universidad Tadeo Lozano.

2012   Individual Club El Nogal

Exposiciones colectivas

1980   St Martins School of Art. Londres.

1981   Final degree Show. St Martins School of Art. Londres.

1982   Arte Colombiano del Siglo XX, Centro Colombo Americano. Bogota.
        Galeria Garces y Velasquez. Bogota. Colombia

1983   Galeria Elida Lara. Barranquilla. Colombia.

1984   Galeria casa Negret. Bogota.

1985   Galeria casa Negret. Bogota.

1985   Exposicion Inaugural, Museo Negret, Popayan. Colombia.

XXXIV Salon Nacional de Artistas. Colcultura, Corferias. Bogota.

Homenaje a Obregon. Galeria el Museo. Bogota.

Art FI 92. Centro de Convenciones Gonzalo Jimenez de Quesada. Bogota.

Doce para un fin de Ano. Centro de Arte Euroamericano. Caracas.

1993 Art Miami 93. Miami Convention Center. Florida.

1994 Art Miami94. Miami Convention Center. Florida.

Art Chicago 94. The new Pier Show, Cityfront Center, Chicago.

1995 Ambrosino Gallery en Art Miami 95, Miami Beach Convention center. Florida.

1996 Mixta. Galeria el Museo. Bogota.

1997 Colectiva. Quinta Galeria. Bogota.

Recreaciones. Centro Colombo Americano. Bogota.

Art Auction. Christie's, Latin American Art. NewYork.

Pequeno Formato. Quinta Galeria. Bogota.

1998 Diez Anos. Galeria el Museo. Bogota.

Generacion Intermedia. Casa de Moneda. Biblioteca Luis Angel Arango. Bogota.

Primer Salon de Arte. Centro de Diseno Portobelo y Galeria el Museo Bogota.

1999 Donacion Banco Cafetero. Banco de Santander. Bogota

Colectiva.Quinta Galeria.Bogota.

1999 Subasta Arte Colombiano del siglo xx. Christie's. Londres

Colectiva. Galeria el Museo. Bogota.

2011   Arte Sacro Galeria Arte 700
2011   Galeria Arte Consultores
2012   Colectiva Estudio Monica Meira
2012   Feria de Arte Houston
2012   Colectiva Abstraccion Esguerra fine art
2013   Feria de Arte en Southampton New York

Colecciones publicas

Museo de Arte Moderno la Tertulia. Cali.

Museo de Arte de la Universidad Nacional. Bogota

Museo de Arte Casa Negret, Popayan. Colombia.

Museo de Arte Latinoamericano. Managua, Nicaragua.

Banco de la República. Biblioteca Luis Angel Arango. Bogota.

Enersis, Santiago de Chile. Museo de la Universidad de Antioquia

D. METTE GAUGUIN

We were unable to find much about Paul Gauguin's great-granddaughter, Mette Gauguin. She has exhibited regularly, a number of European Gauguin's mentioned her art, and we came across her in our research. We found two interviews in 2011 which revealed more about her grandfather than her.

Paul Rogers' interview focused largely on Mette's reactions to her great-grandfather's (Paul Gauguin) perceived sexual peccadillos. It seems that if you are famous you will be attacked in the name of investigative reporting and freedom of speech. But this leaves the surviving descendants shouldering the opprobrium. http://www.independent.co.uk/arts-entertainment/art/news/gauguins-british-relative-disputes-artists-notoriety-2191988.html#

Christine Riding's interview also focused on Paul: Mette's perceptions of her great- grandfather but the interview has pizazz. With smart insights she discussed his painting technique making interesting comments about his brush strokes, paint thickness, color and the Tate's (museum) marvelous display of his works. http://www.tate.org.uk/context-comment/blogs/exclusive-interview-gauguins-great-grand-daughter

Sadly, as we learned about Emile, Mette Gauguin's career has become overshadowed by her great-grandfather. Also, she had the misfortune to have the same name as Paul Gauguin's wife and her second cousin. There is some indication that she is also a printmaker, too, but alas we were unable to find any example of her works on the internet. She does have a Facebook page but it contains no examples. We have tried to contact her

2. GENEALOGIES

A. FIGURE 1: DESCENDANTS OF EMILE GAUGUIN AND OLGA VON HEDEMANN
(a continuation of Figure 1 in Chapter 1)

A. Aline Gauguin *09.12.1909
- a. Jeanne Henriette Honore
    1. Jakob Nielsen
    2. Kamilla Nielsen
        - A. Anna Baagø
        - B. Jakob Boaag
    3. Andreas Brendholt

B. Børge Emile Gauguin *20.04.1911 (My father)
- a. Michala Gauguin – died at seven by allied bombs near WWII end
- b. Aline Gauguin
    1. Michael Houghton-Larsen
        - A. Nicolas H-L
        - B. Jonathan H-L
    2. Christian Houghton-Larsen
        - A. Caroline H-L
        - B. Davil H-L
    3. Thomas Houghton-Larsen
        - A. Rie H-L
        - B. Theodor H-L

3. Sophie Gauguin
    A. Olivia Astrid Dahl Gauguin
    B. Wilma Maria Dahl Gauguin
f. Emile Gauguin
C. Pedro Maria Gauguin, *24.10.1913
a. Marianne Gauguin

Mar 24, 2007

Hi all,

Thanx for all these nice mails from hopefully new friends.

I do not know where to start or where to end. But let me introduce the Danish family tree of Emile Gauguin. We have a lot of data, unfortunately most of it is not readily available on digital form yet.

We have a fair amount of information about the ancestors of Emile going all the way back to year 736!!!. However, as there are no children of the "old" Emile alive and as (I think) none of my sisters and my brother ever saw Emile, it is going to be a challenge to find any information. But let us try. The oldest family member still alive (?) is Jeanne (*29.04.1933) but I have no contact to her, but that could of course change.

That's all for now

Philippe

   5Jeronimo Vila Holguin
   5Antonia Vila Holguin
  4Julian Vila Holguin & Daniela Angel
   5Mateo Vila Angel
  4Maria Uribe Echeverri
  4Lina Uribe Echeverri & Ricardo Brubaker
 3Pedro Echeverri Uribe & Pilar Mejia
  4Natalia Echeverri Mejia & Juan Jose Abeddrabo
  4Catalina Echeverri Mejia
  4Juan Carlos Echeverri Mejia
 3Emma Echeverri Uribe & Juan Agustin Angel
  4Tatiana Angel Echeverri
  4Luis Guillermo Angel Echeverri
 3Enrique Echeverri Uribe & Margarita Pinzon
  4Nicolas Echeverri Pinzon
2Margot Uribe Gauguin Torres (1921-2016) & Hernando Uribe-Holguin Uribe (1909-1972), married 1945 (see Figure 2C, Photographs II)
 (NOTE: Margot's name was also spelled Margoth but still pronounced 'Margo'.)
 3Pedro Miguel Uribe-Holguin Uribe (1945-1996) & Maria Victoria Gomez
  4Paula Uribe Gomez (1972-) & Hernando Quinones
   5Hernando Quinones Uribe
   5Miguel Quinones Uribe
  4Nicolas Uribe Gomez & Alicia Lozano Vila
   5Benjamin Uribe Lozano

3Juan Pablo Uribe Arango †
3Mauricio Uribe Arango & Pilar Donatiu
    4Pilar Uribe Donatiu
    4Paula Uribe Donatiu
2Gloria Uribe Gauguin Torres & Carlos Ortiz
    3Juan Carlos Ortiz Uribe & Maria Teresa Rueda
        4Alexandra Ortiz Rueda & Diego Dorado (3 children)
        4Andres Ortiz Rueda & Pilar Naves
        4Marcela Ortiz Rueda
    3Silvia Ortiz Uribe & Jose Lloreda Londono
        4Viviana Lloreda Ortiz & Andres Maldonado
            5Carmen Maldonado Lloreda
            5Jose Maldonado Lloreda
        4Felipe Lloreda Ortiz
        4Cristina Lloreda Ortiz & Mauricio Ibanez
            5Sylvia de Dios Ibanez Lloreda
            5Maria de la Paz Ibanez Lloreda
            5Diana de la Mar Ibanez Lloreda
        4Carlos Jose Lloreda Ortiz & Estefania Neme
            5Salvador Lloreda Neme
    3Maria Clara Ortiz Uribe † & Rodrigo Escobar
        4Gloria Elena Escobar Ortiz & Federico Cabrera
            5Clara Cabrera Escobar
            5Miguel Cabrera Escobar
            5Pablo Cabrera Escobar
        4Diana Escobar Ortiz & Juan Carlos Monzon
            5Gabriela Monzon Escobar

4Andrea McAllister Ortiz

3Maria Isabel Ortiz Uribe & Rafael Klug

4Maria Klug Ortiz

4Daniel Klug Ortiz

4Tatiana Klug Ortiz

3Ines Elvira Ortiz Uribe & Diego Ortiz

4Martin Ortiz Ortiz

4Mariana Ortiz Ortiz

2Clara Estela Uribe Gauguin Torres & Enrique Piedrahita Currea

3Enrique Piedrahita Uribe (1956-) & Luisa Fernanda Tamayo

4Elena Piedrahita Tamayo

4Luis Fernando Piedrahita Tamayo

3Elena Piedrahita Uribe (1958 -) & Guillermo Venegas Klinge

4Adriana Venegas Piedrahita

4Andres Venegas Piedrahita

4Rafael Venegas Piedrahita

4Maurico Venegas Piedrahita

3Ana Lucia Piedrahita Uribe (1960 -) & Alejandro Rengifo

4 Pedro Rengifo Piedrahita

4Juliana Rengifo Piedrahita

3Rafael Piedrahita Uribe (1974 -) & Marta Patricia Di Terlizzi

4Maria Andrea Piedrahita Di Terlizzi

4Lina Piedrahita Di Terlizzi

     5Paula Urrutia Albrecht

     5Martin Urrutia Albrecht

     5Daniel Urrutia Albrecht

     5Julien Urrutia Albrecht

    4Pablo Urrutia Escobar & Claudia Montoya

     5Tomas Urrutia Montoya

     5Samuel Urrutia Montoya

  3Felipe Escobar Uribe & Olga Lucia Herrera, 1st wife; & Olga Lucia Lozano 2nd wife; & Patricia Höher, 3rd wife. Note: each wife bore a single child.

    4Alejandra Escobar Herrera

    4Alvaro Escobar Lozano

    4Laura Escobar Höher †

2Consuelo Uribe-Holguin (1904-1913) Her ashes are interred sometime after 2000 with her grandparents Juan Nepomuceno Uribe and Marie Gauguin de Uribe in the Uribe mausoleum.

2Juan Uribe-Holguin Uribe (1903-1983) & Margarita Holguin Nieto (1905-1977)

  3Consuelo Uribe-Holguin Holguin (1930-00) & Manuel Jose Iriarte de la Torre (1923-57) 1st husband; & Luis Felipe Suarez Williamson (1933-) 2nd husband

    4Carmen Iriarte Uribe-Holguin (1954 -) & Fabricio Robledo Cuellar (1960 -)

     5Camilo Robledo Iriarte (1987-)

     5Daniel Robledo Iriarte (1990-)

     5Nicolas Robledo Iriarte (1992 -)

5Alejandro Cuellar Suarez (1985 -)

4Rosario Suarez Uribe-Holguin (1958 -)

3Emilia Uribe-Holguin Holguin (1937 - 2010) & Rafael Perez Norzagaray (- 2010)

    4Cristian Perez Uribe-Holguin (1961-) & Diana Quijano Becerra

    4Emilia Perez Uribe-Holguin (1962-) & Bernardo Rodriguez Ossa

    4Laura Perez Uribe-Holguin (1963-)

3Pilar Uribe-Holguin Holguin (1940-) & Roberto Aparicio Gomez Davila †

    4Nicolas Aparicio Uribe-Holguin (1963 -) & Pamela Kornye

        5 Nicolas Aparicio Kornye (1994 -)

        5 Gabriela Aparicio Kornye (1996 - 2013)

    4Pilar Aparicio Uribe-Holguin (1964 -)

    4Elvira Carmen Aparicio Uribe-Holguin (1967 -)

2Beatriz Uribe-Holguin Uribe † & Eusebio Umana †

    3Juan Manuel Umana Uribe & Luisa de Brigard, 1st wife; & Paulina _____ 2nd wife

    4Juanita Umana _____

    4Beatriz Umana _____

    4Carlos Umana _____

2Hernando Uribe-Holguin Uribe (1909-1972) & Margot Uribe-Gauguin Torres

(1921-2016) Their children are listed in Fig 2A

2Mercedes Uribe-Holguin Uribe † & Juan B. Tobar †

4Avaro Perez Uribe
4Cristina Perez Uribe

Figures 2 A-C Notes: Marie Gauguin and Juan Nepomuceno Uribe had three children: first, fraternal twins, Pedro and Carmen who were born in 1879 and a year later Maria Elena was born (Sweetman gave the dates a year earlier and switched the birth order). Juan was 30 and Marie was 32 when Pedro and Carmen were born (see Photographs II for childhood pictures). We concluded that Carmen died in France, since only Pedro and Maria Elena accompanied their mother to Colombia. When Emile arrived there in Bogota at age 26 his aunt was 53, her husband, Juan, had already died and his cousins Pedro and Maria Elena were 21 and 20, respectively.

We have listed all the children of Juan and Marie as three lineages: the Pedro Uribe line of the family as Figure 2A, his twin sister Carmen as Figure 2B and the lineage of their sister Maria Elena as Figure 2C. The Arabic number in front of a name is the generation ("1" is the first generation in this case the children of Juan and Marie, "2" means Juan and Marie's grandchildren, "3" would be great grandchildren etc. The symbol "&" indicates marriage; in the diagram, the single, vertical line"|" means a single child, a "/\" refers to twins, and the "†" symbol indicates deceased but no date of death. Dates in parentheses indicate birth and death dates where available.

Figure 2 A–C unlike the other two genealogies, Figures 1, 3 and Emile's (presented by grandson Philippe above), uses the Hispanic naming protocol which preserves the

http://www.ciudadviva.gov.co/portal/node/160 its March 6, 2013 and http://es.wikipedia.org/wiki/Emile_Gauguin. One of the photographs was of a burial urn cemented into a wall of the Iglesia Santa Clara in Bogota with the names of ashes of those entombed: "Juan N Uribe Buenaventura 1845-1894, Marie Gauguin de Uribe 1846-1918, and Consuelo Uribe-Holguin 1904-1913". The information provided by the family had Juan Nepomuceno's death in 1896, and although no one was aware of the inscription on the burial urn, we do have his death certificate which clearly and unequivocally gives his death date as 1896. It was a transcriptional error by the craftsman who relabeled the urn after Marie's death. Juan N. lived a short life, but there is no reason why we should make it shorter. Great-great-grandson Juan Nicolas recently informed us that their ashes have now been moved to the Uribe mausoleum at the Central Cemetery of Bogota.

We knew Juan and Marie, but who was Consuelo? She did not appear in any of the family trees we inspected. Who were her parents? We concluded that she was a daughter of Maria Elena and Miguel, and we have included her as such in lineage Fig. 2 C in the family tree. She has her father's name (Uribe-Holguin) and her birthdate lies within the birthdates of her brothers and sisters that are known (those of the other six children are unknown). We do not know when Maria Elena and Miguel married but we do we know the birth dates of four of her ten children ranging from 1903 to 1909. Consuelo's birth falls within this bracket. The fact that two of the children were born in 1903 suggests that there was a transcriptional error,

family married Blanca Williamson who appears not follow the Hispanic name-order rule. There is evidence that Emile communicated with Blanca and may have visited each other. Great-granddaughter Consuelo Uribe-Holguin Holguin remarried a man named Luis Felipe Suarez Williamson who might be the brother of Alberto Suarez Williamson. It is possible that they are related to their aunt Blanca Williamson. Also the names Uribe and Holguin, both common in Colombia, have entered the family several times.

SOURCES

A preliminary genealogy of Emile's Aunt Marie by Francisco Javier Manuel Carbone Montes from his website (below) played a crucial role in learning about Emile's life in Colombia and his early years in the US. (http://gw13.geneanet.org/fracarbo?lang=es;pz=francisco+javier+manuel;nz=carbone+montes;ocz=0;p=marie;n=gauguin+chazal).

Thanks to Mr. Carbon through his colleague and fellow genealogist Mr. Chacon we were able to locate living Uribe-Gauguin family members, particularly Margot Torres Uribe Gauguin, Juan Nicolas Uribe-Holguin Uribe, and Carmen Iriarte Uribe-Holguin who provided us with details to complete the modern family tree. Tragically Sr. Carbone passed away during the creation of this project which we have dedicated to his memory. In addition we are grateful for helpful genealogical details from works of Sweetman and J.M. Roca and A.H. Riise.

C. Figure 3: Descentants Of Axel Malm And Alma Meincke (By Dr. Ole Secher, Relative Of Bitten Jensen)

1Alma Meincke (1883 - 1976) & Axel Malm (1884 -1947)
    2Pier Malm (1906-) & Sylvia Malm (19-)
        3Sylvia Malm (1948-) adopted two girls when she was 50.
    2Edmee Malm (1911 - 1947) & Charles Elliott Loughlin (1910-1989)
        3Edmee Kay (1936 - 2012) & Woody Ryan (m.1959)
        3Lynn (1937-) & Theodore Higgins (1936 - 1964)
            4Deborah Higgins
            4Katherin Higgins
            Lynn remarried with Ernest Duvall (1925 -) and had no children.
1Ellen Meincke (1874-1956) & Edvard Jensen (1865-1919)
    2Else Jensen (1898-1973) & John (Jack) Foster Bass II (189-) (m. 1927)
        3 John F Bass III (Johnny) & Barbara Avildsen
            4John F Bass IV & Cathy Cifers, 1st wife †; & Kathy Sulkowski, 2nd wife
    2Niels Jensen (1902-1982) & Lisa Lowe Jensen (1903-1999)
        3Helle Bitten Jensen (1929-) & Robert Krentel (19- - 2015)
            4Lisa Krentel (1951-)
            4Julie Krentel (1955-)
            4Katherine Krentel (1956-)
            4Robert Krentel (1964-)

Emile and Priscilla Gauguin. Her son Niels who married Lisa also had a single child, Helle Bitten Jensen who became friends with Kate Butterworth and provided helpful suggestions and information for the book including this family tree. Bitten Jensen (married name: Krentel) who was born in 1929 lived for a while with the Malm's in Plymouth Meeting and when she was eight they all moved to North Wales. Before moving to Plymouth Meeting, the Jensen's lived in Washington DC where Niels had a surveying business. At the start of World War II Niels was recruited as an engineer with Lukens Steel Company that made steel plates for the US Navy. His story is one of thousands as the US geared up for the incredible, na-tionwide, industrial production buildup to fight Germany and Japan. The factory was about 35 miles away from North Wales in Coatesville, PA, and the plates were transported to ship-yards on the coast. In 1940 the Jensen's moved to Glenmoor, PA, closer to Coatesville. Many years later Niels retired from Lukens as head engineer.

Bitten married Robert Krentel, had four children and is the recipient of Emile's only surviving artwork, a decorated, wooden spool (daughter Lisa an artist, photographed Emile's spool). Her sister Elsa married into the Kirk family and had two children, one, Niels Kirk died in a car crash.

Ellen and Edvard had two more children both born in Denmark: Jydde Jensen, who knew Emile and Priscilla when they lived in Florida. Knud Jensen lived in New Jersey.

John Foster Bass II joined the Malm-Jensen clan in 1927 when he married Bitten Jensen's Aunt Else and they became

3. EUROPEAN GAUGUIN EMAIL EXCHANGE

[During the research phase of this project we sought input from Emile's relatives by posing questions to them. What resulted was recollections and comments from Clovis, Gauguin, Philippe Gauguin, Mette Gauguin Fonseca, and Jacques Gauguin; Jacques children, Jonas Gauguin and Michala Gauguin; and Bitten Jensen Krentel in response to inquiries from the authors. As you can read they did not have the benefit of our research, then, and their beginning assumptions, as ours, were entirely wrong.]

Sent: Tuesday, March 27, 2007 9:46 AM Clovis wrote
Hi David !

It seems that spring has come to Denmark with the sun and warm. I'm glad that Philippe has joined the conversation, because he knows a little more about his grandfather (Emile) than I do. I know of course a lot about my grandfather because I knew him and saw him nearly every day until he died. It was actually he, who turned me on to be a silversmith and always cheered me to be creative. My father got really pissed when I told him that I wanted to be a silversmith and not a civil engineer, and we didn't speak with each other for a couple of years. But when I finished my education and had a medal of honor for my masterpiece by the Danish king, he accepted that I have chosen to go an artistic way and not an academic like himself. I think that the decedents of PG have two sides in them. The straight and the freak side. But because of PGs reputation and fame, they think twice before they jump on the artistic/freak side.

I still think it is a pity, that I never received Priscilla's ring. Look out for it!!!

In one of the documents a Mother Ellen is mentioned. I am sure she came to Denmark with lots of greeting from Emile and Priscilla, and that my older sister, Aline, saw her and accompanied her for a day or even more. I will try to get some information about this from my sister. But she is ill and may not remember.

I have been too busy to find the documents I have promised you, but I will certainly do it before X-mass.

You have asked me, if I don't think it was odd, that grandma' Olga never took interest in us. Yes, it is odd, but she and my mother didn't get along very well, and I think that my mother has been very much an obstacle to her seeing us. Still, I remember when I was a young girl I spent once or twice a week in her little flat in Copenhagen, and in another one in Lyngby (just outside Copenhagen). And I have good memory of her. She suffered from asthma, and now and then, when we were walking, she would stop and use her inhalator, and then go on again. She was not the kind that hugged and kissed, but she was nice.

Thank you, again, and congratulations on your paintings. I myself have done a few, too, but not lately.

Friendliest regards.

Mette Gauguin Fonseca

Mette Fonseca wrote again:

Dear David:

I think I started to write to my grandfather as soon as I could write. I know that my sister Aline wrote to him regularly,

exciting to receive a package from America. They would send us Christmas presents and things they knew we were short of after WWII. I especially remember coffee beans that my mother roasted on a pan over a fire. All of the house would be filled with the delicious scent of coffee.

I can also tell you a funny little story that Emile's daughter, Aline, used to tell about her parents' last meeting when my grandfather came to visit his children in Copenhagen. EG was climbing the stairs to the third floor where they lived and my grandmother leaned out to see him. Her greeting was "Hi Emile, you look much older", to which he answered, looking up to see her "And you look much heavier"!

If I had known that you also took an interest in Emile's life with Olga, I would have sent some more pictures for Philippe to give to you from when they were still in South America, along with a copy of the most wonderful old document, namely the passport of Olga along with a photo of she and her children. She was a very beautiful lady, and was a noble woman, but when married to a "plebian" (EG) the rest of our family lost the nobility. I think that our branch (his eldest son EG, Jr. and us) were the only ones who had regular contact with him. My father's brother, Pedro Maria, never wrote as far as I know. My Aunt Aline went to stay with him in Philadelphia (before Florida) for some months (maybe a whole year) and worked in some hospital as a nurse. She was a midwife but served as a nurse. I should have paid closer attention to her when she babbled about her stay with her father. I might have written to him now and then.

"Polyteknisk Laereanstalt)". If we have to be positive about his studies, he could be considered a bachelor in engineering, when he set out to Bogota, Colombia, and South America to head a division of a road-building company. The general opinion was, that he was successful in his work. My grandmother, Olga von Hedemann was not extremely happy about his career. She pendled back and forth between Denmark and Colombia and thus had the first child, Aline (B. 1909) in Colombia, my father 1911 in Copenhagen and the last of the three siblings, Pedro Maria in Colombia1913.

The arrival of PM, who was almost lost in poor hygienic conditions during the delivery also gave her the final inspiration to leave Emile for good, or at least to settle for herself in Copenhagen. She never remarried. I know her from my childhood as a very bitter and self-centered person.

The story of Emile, that I like most is, that during the 30'es in the US he formed a cooperation with a Swedish engineer, name unknown. Because of the economic depression, the World did not need much engineering consultation, but the two of them had to make a living of their combined skills. Since they both were around 2 meters in height and thus a bit scaring in physical appearance, they offered a service as "money-collectors". The story goes, that they had many clients since they were rather successful in convincing (or threatening?) people to pay their debt.

I have never been able to figure out if it is one of my father stories about his father or if it really happened. As far as I know, Emile actually cooperated with a Swedish engineer at some point. But it is not easy to tell the truth of the story.

father and perhaps a similar personality, irritated Mette Gad so much that it could have soured their relationship. It must have been a very sad (angry) environment in their house at that time because of the recent deaths of Aline and Clovis. Philippe showed photos of EG and his two surviving brothers as mature adults when I was in Copenhagen and it is striking how much alike all three looked.

I was divorced when my three children were in their teens but continued to support them (financially/emotionally) and lived nearby to maintain a close relationship to this day. All three plus two spouses, one four-year-old grandson, two dogs and my ex-wife will be staying at my house for four days over Christmas. I mention this because I wonder if EG continued to financially support his three children from America? Other than his daughter, Aline visiting in 1946, did any of EG's other children visit him in America? (I agree and appreciate how diff-icult/ expensive a transatlantic trip at that time would be). Did your father ever correspond with his father?

The total financial/emotional burden of raising three children alone could account for some of the "bitterness" Olga felt. No doubt similar to that felt by her mother-in-law, Mette Gad. Wonder if the two "abandoned" women shared their anger with each other over afternoon tea during the last two years of Mette's life (1918-1920)?

I knew that Olga's maiden name was Hedemann, but you added "Von". That prefix in German could indicate an upper-class family. Would that apply to a Danish name as well? Wonder if Olga's "roots" were in the Danish side of Schleswig-Holstein?

This means that although the family was poor it had the right connections.

It is said, that Emile belonged to a historically famous "club" of young gentlemen who "toured" the night life of Copenhagen. One of the members is said to be the Danish King-to-be, Christian X. These gentlemen had at least one thing in common: their excessive physical height. All of them were around 2 meters. I was told that they even named themselves "The Two Meter Club". Considered the social reality at that time (1890s) it was unthinkable that the club would include Emile if he had not been considered a nobleman.

So my interpretation of these details is that Emile slightly overestimated his own talents and skills, although this may have been less obvious in his later days.

My family had regular, but only postal connection with him during the late 1940'es and early 1950'es until he died.

My impression is that Priscilla was the one who cared for his family. At least the broken connection was reestablished at the time when she became his wife.

Turning back to the von Hedemann's, this family originated in Germany as a rather insignificant German noble family. They emigrated and arrived in Denmark as far as I know in the first half of 19th century. This is actually not unusual in Denmark. So if it is a "German" trait, to be aware of one's value as a consequence of the family. This goes for quite a number of Danes.

Summarizing: It was an unequal marriage not mainly in social level, but as well in view upon adventure, roles, expectations etc.

Jan 23 2008. Jonas Gauguin wrote

Can't really see why this needs a woman's perspective, but I've cc Michala my bigger sister and now colleague, too.
In my world this just looks like EG having the situation where you get married with children and then suddenly realizes you haven't lived your life out. Olga trying to talk sense to the bachelor-kinda-dude (EG) for the last time, but fails & returns to DK. Happens a lot. My father has always had other women than my mother, now living with his third wife ;)

Jan 26, 2008 Mette Gauguin Fonseca wrote
Hi David,

I know I am not writing to you as much as you could wish, but I have been down with a bad flue, that I caught in cold Denmark.

It is news to me that Olga's mother, Elisabeth Henriette Riise, also went to the US. I will ask one of my cousins, descendants of Olga's sister Ellen, if they know anything about it. After all Olga's mother is their great-grandmother, too.

I know, though, that Emile accepted to pay a monthly alimony to Olga, and it was, as far as I remember typed immediately after the signatures of the contract he had made with the employer. Aline, Olga's daughter, wrote underneath: "Mom never saw a penny!" If I find his document, I will send you a copy.

I have a small part of Olga Gauguin's memories. It is about a trip she made, when she was 16 years old, with her mother and sister, to St. Thomas, where they visited the new owner of "Pharmacy A.H.Riise", the son of A.H. Riise and brother of Olga's mother. I can translate it, if you find it interesting. It

of an ancient, though famous, ancestor, secondly because the interaction between members of the family has not in the present 4-6 generations after PG been very close.

A third viewpoint, which contradicts the hypothesis of common family personality, is that defining common traits in a complex environment could be considered a well-known human behaviour: To simplify the very complex matter of formation of personality in order to experience a better understanding.

Personally I do not find a discussion about an (unchangeable) personality meaningful.

But If you guys find it useful - please continue. I shall patiently read your comments. If I change my opinion on the subject, I will comment.

Until then: Have some nice days and mail discussions.

Cordially Jacques

Pariah among full-bred Gauguins - simply: Myself.

January 27 Mette wrote to David.

Hi David

I just saw again that you would like to have comments on the high statistic of the Gauguin's divorce rate. Either the men left their wives and children; or the wives left their husbands and took their children with them.

For me to see it is because the Gauguin men are very charming, but also very unfaithful, and only few women can cope with that.

On the other hand, who am I to comment on this subject?

I think that all Gauguin's, men and women, are prepared to fight for what they really think is right no matter the consequences.

So long. Mette

Feb 9, 2008 Michala Gauguin answered David

Hi David,

No I haven't read the book. But I have it (I think) in Norwegian. At least it is a book called "Paul Gauguin" by Pola. One of my patients gave it to me a couple of years ago, while I was still working in hospitals. Unfortunately I have only read scientific articles for a long time.

Regarding the Preface, I do not think it is sympathetic (as I read it) but quite neutral in his choice of words. If he was sympathetic regarding his father, he would have started with something like "to my beloved father or in memorial of my beloved father" or something like that! But it could also be strictly business, who wants to read a book about a jerk??? (Unless, of course, it is a biography of a psychotic serial killer!)

He probably did not know his father very well, so this could be the reason for writing the Preface that is so "fluffy".

But I do not know a lot about him and/or his relationship to his father, I am too young to have experienced the atmosphere in the home of my grandfather/grandmother!

This is only a suggestion.

I can, by the way, recommend you to read the book "Xenophobes Guide to Danes" it is a quite funny book and describes Danish people very well. (I have read it myself, since

The Bass' only child was Johnny who was my contemporary. His son, John, now lives in Englewood as well as his wife Kathy. Mother Ellen was my grandmother as well as Charlie Hegener's, and John's great-grandmother. They all lived on the property when Priscilla and Emile lived there and should remember much.

This is a wonderful project. I only wish I give you more information.

Bitten Krentel nee. Helle Lowe Jensen

Mette wrote David McIntyre November 9, 2008.

Hi David,

Olga was not well off. She had some help from the family, but she also worked at the Ministry of War for quite a long period of years. There was not chance of government help. Nothing like that existed at the time, and she wold probably not have used it if there were: I think she would have been too proud. Yes, she struggled and was furious that Emile never sent her a cent. As it seems, it was because he did not want to. I think he was angry that she divorced him. In that context, I think he was an optimist about his brilliant future, as his father, trying to drag in the whole family through his adventures. In the family, the wives of the Gauguin men have always said that the Gauguin have "the mania of greatness". We think we are something special. It is true, more of less, for many of us that we come from the Kings of Portugal, France etc. and from various Popes, why shouldn't we feel special?

Well, enough about philosophy.

4. TIMELINE OF THE FAMILIES AND PEOPLE

[Note: the Hispanic names have this order: first the given name(s), then the father's last name, then, finally the mother's last name.]

1773-1859/60	Juan Pio de Tristan, uncle of Flora Tristan (his death year is not clear).
1797-1860	Andre Francois Chazal Buterne is born, future husband of Flora Tristan.
1803-1844	Flora Tristan was born April 7 in Paris (Vaugirard), France, died at 41 in Bordeaux. She was Emile Gauguin's paternal, great-grandmother.
1814 -1849	Guillaume Clovis Pierre Gauguin Juranville. Known as Clovis, Aline's husband and father of Marie and Paul, died on the trip to Peru.
1818-1883	Gustave Arosa, financier, art collector, protector of the young Gauguin family, first meeting in 1861.
1821	Flora Tristan at 18 married Andre Francois Chazal Buterne at 24.
1825-1867	Aline Chazal Gauguin was born in October, died at 42 in Paris, Emile Gauguin's paternal grandmother.
1835	Flora Tristan's first book, *Peregrinations of a Pariah* was published. See a list of her publications in below in the Appendix.
1838	Flora Tristan was wounded by husband, Andre Chazal.

1879-1966	Pedro Uribe Gauguin was born in Paris, died in Bogota.
1879	Carmen Uribe Gauguin, Pedro's twin sister was born in Paris, died very young in Paris.
1880-1947	Maria Elena Uribe Gauguin was born in Paris, died in Bogota.
1880	Emile Gauguin is sent to Copenhagen to be well educated.
1881-1961	Jean Rene Gauguin, Emile's brother was born in Paris, died in Denmark.
1882-1967	Olga von Hedemann, Emile's first wife was born in Copenhagen, died in Denmark.
1883-1961	Paul Rollon "Pola" Gauguin, Emile's brother, was born in Paris, died in Denmark.
1883	Paul Gauguin for the first time declared himself an "artist" on Pola's official birth registration.
1883	Gustave Arosa died.
1885	Paul and Mette Gauguin and family moved to Copenhagen, reunited with Emile.
1885	Paul took Clovis at age 6 back to Paris with him.
1891	Paul Gauguin visited his family in Copenhagen, the last time.
1891	Emile entered the Polytechnic School.
1893	Marie Gauguin de Uribe with her children arrived in Bogota, Colombia.
1896	Juan Nepomuceno Uribe Buenaventura died in Bogota.

1918	Marie Gauguin Uribe died in Bogota.
1920	Mette Sophia Gad Gauguin died in Denmark.
1920	Emile's census report showed he lived in Lower Meriam Township, PA.
1921	Emile published Preface to *Paul Gauguin's Intimate Journals* and authorized publication of *Noa Noa*.
1923	Emile became a US Citizen on June 25.
1937	February 18 Emile returned from Denmark after reconciliation III with Olga failed.
1938	Emile wrote the 30-page letter to Maria Elena Uribe.
1939	Emile and Priscilla met.
1940	Emile Gauguin (66) married Priscilla Buntin (44) in Philadelphia.
1946	Aline Gauguin visited Priscilla and Emile for a year.
1935-2013	Mette Fonseca Gauguin, granddaughter of Emile was born in Denmark and died in Portugal.
1947	Maria Elena Uribe Gauguin died in Bogota at age 67.
1949-2015	Clovis Henri Gauguin, son of Pierre, grandson of Jean Rene, was born in Denmark.
1950	Philippe Gauguin, Emile's grandson was born in Denmark.
1950	Emile and Priscilla, moved to Englewood, Florida for retirement.

5. Miscelaneous

A. Commentary on Emile's Wikipedia article

The Wikipedia article on Emile (http://es.wikipedia.org/wiki/Emile_Gauguin) was ample evidence that his memory lived on 115 years later). Generally memories fade, but memories of him appear to have remained bright. It only rarely refers to his Colombian family other than his Aunt Marie and his Uncle Juan's antimalarial drug (quinine) business. Although the article does contain much information about Paul Gauguin and his life, we cannot comment, but only refer you to other biographical works about Paul for corroboration.

We asked ourselves just how popular to readers Emile's article was in comparison let's say to Colombia's warrior and statesman General Rafael Reyes (http://en.wikipedia.org/wiki/Rafael_Reyes). Created by Erik7 in 2007 with 58 people adding editorial changes and information up until 2015 with about 1588 views in a recent 90-day period. In comparison Emile's site had a total of 24 people working on it with 346 visits over the same time period. Although Emile was only 1/5 as popular, it was still impressive

Because Wikipedia articles are not always composed by historians with credentials to uphold, accuracy has to be questioned. One way to be assured of accuracy is the reference citations. In the Emile article they are poor. Few led to

from Latin America. These people include painters, philosophers, sculptors, writers, journalists, revolutionaries, explorers, and one other engineer. Go to: https://es.wikipedia.org/wiki/Usuario:Juan_Fabio He also has created 18 Wikipedia articles about places and topics including the history of Peru and the novel *Moon and Six Pence* by Somerset Maugham. He has a pointed interest in Sogamoso because he also has created brief pages about the Spanish discoverer of Sogamoso (Juan de San Martin) and Myths and Legends of Sogamoso, Hymns and Anthems of Sogamoso, Shields of Sogamoso, the Anthropological Museum of Sogamoso, and the History of Sogamoso. His serious focus on Sogamoso, suggests he lives in or spent significant time there; and that may have been key in writing about the son of a famous painter.

The reason that we are going into such detail about Juan Fabio's achievements Wikipedia-wise is that we might learn how he developed an attraction to Emile. Juan Fabio's interests it seems are very broad and not focused on any one person or thing. For example research on Maugham's novel about Paul Gauguin may have led his interest to Emile and fellow Colombian. He does refer to a conversation with Eduardo Barrera Garcia who may have published something about Emile that might be in a Sogamoso library, perhaps the Biblioteca Joaquin Camargo. A preliminary, online search on the library website for Emilo Gauguin or Eduardo Barrera Garcia yielded nothing. So with Juan Fabio's concern with lesser known personalities he sees a need to educate us about these important yet unrecognized

B. COMMENTARY ON JUAN MANUEL ROCA ARTICLE

In Emile's Wikipedia article we cited in various places in the narrative an article (www.ciudadviva.gov.co/portal/node/160 by Colombian poet and author, Juan Manuel Roca, about the Uribe-Gauguin family. In a breezy, chatty manner, speckled with untranslatable metaphors he wrote about Gauguin and Uribe trivia. Briefly it alluded to four topics of interest we covered in the narrative: a. the speculation that Simon Bolivar genes lie in the Tristan-Gauguin lineage, b. the Uribe family's attempts to verify six, Paul Gauguin landscapes, c. the inadvertent discovery of a missing Gauguin-Uribe descendant, and d. how Marie Gauguin de Uribe moved her children and their belongings to Bogota.

First, we are confident that we have put an end to the erroneous speculation that Aline Chazal Gauguin was fathered by Simon Bolivar (see Table I in Chapter 2). Second, Juan Nicolas Uribe and Cristian Perez Uribe showed us photos of two paintings that were verified as Paul Gauguin originals described in Chapters 1 and 6. We guessed that these two works may be among the six Roca mentioned. Next, Roca unknowingly revealed a missing Gauguin descendant, Consuelo Uribe-Holguin, Marie Gauguin's granddaughter whose ashes rested in a family burial urn in the Santa Clara Church in Bogota. The ashes of Juan N., Marie and Consuelo now, we were told by Juan Nicolas, have been moved to the Uribe mausoleum at the Central Cemetery of Bogota. We identified her with the help of Carmen Iriarte Uribe in Chapter 4 and the Uribe family

"My father's family was displaced from their huge farms and extensive land was taken from them.

"Also, I have an aunt (not blood related) who was "given" to my father's family when she was nine years old by her mom, who was also displaced and couldn't support her. Eventually this aunt reunited with her sister (who was given to another family) after almost 60 years!

"So, of course it affected many families at the time, as well as the violence, and displacement affects thousands of people still."

Alfredo's story:

"I don't remember many specific stories my dad or any other family member mentioned. The ones I heard from my dad were during that period when sympathizers of the Conservador party or "Godos", as they used to be called, went house-to-house looking to kill members of the Liberal party. My grandma had to hide with my dad under her bed and prayed they were not found. When they left, she got my dad and left the little town for a safer place to live. My dad's pueblo was in the Department of Boyaca.

"And on my mom's side the day of El Bogotazo, April 9 of 1948, she used to tell me that my grandparents had to keep my older uncles, teenagers at the time, locked in the house because they wanted to go downtown Bogota to see for themselves what the people did, burning cable cars,

for the loss of his ear. There has been much speculation how it happened. The most common explanation is that it was removed by the artist himself. One story that comes to mind, is that a prostitute named Rachel called him a silly goose. In a drunken rage he sliced off an ear and gave it to her, wrapped in a blood-soaked newspaper saying that now he was a real goose. Others claimed the self-mutilation was that he was in a deranged state caused by his underlying mental illness where there was no shortage of diagnoses from epilepsy to bipolar disorder to Meniere's disease (causing a painful tinnitus in the ear). Still others asserted that van Gogh's mental state was influenced by external causes such as alcoholism, becoming poisoned by the heavy metals in his paints or the mercury in his syphilis medication.

Sweetman in his excellent 1995 biography gives a very detailed account of the Arles association in 11 pages. And Martin Gayford in 2006 expanded these pages into an entire book, *The Yellow House: Van Gogh and Gauguin and Nine Turbulent Weeks in Provence*. The biographies described vivid and violent scenes involving the two men culminating with the bloody event at Christmastime. Sweetman does not speculate as to the cause but notes that van Gogh was alone at the time since Gauguin decided to stay that night in a hotel leaving us to conclude that van Gogh did the cutting.

However, a carefully researched book by Kaufman and Wildegans (2008) *Van Gogh's Ear: Paul Gauguin and the Pact*

6. WORKS BY AND ABOUT FLORA TRISTAN

A good place to start in your exploration of Flora's works is a potpourri of excerpts, *Flora Tristan, Utopian Feminist*, selected, translated and edited by Doris Beik and Paul Beik, published 1993, Indiana University Press, Bloomington. Included in it are excerpts from, *Women Travelers, Peregrinations of a Pariah, Mephis, Promenades in London, Workers' Union, The Tour of France* (published almost in its entirety). You have already read one quote from the latter in Chapter 2.

1. *Peregrinations of a Pariah*, by Flora Tristan (Originally published, 1835) and Jean Hawkes, translator/editor (Current edition, 1985), Virago Press, London.

2. *The Workers' Union* by Flora Tristan (originally published in 1843) and Beverly Livingston, Translator/editor (current edition 2007), University of Illinois Press, Urbana. This was her manifesto, wrote Jean Hawkes, containing many of the ideas of Karl Marx' *Manifesto* published, 1848.

3. *Tour de France*, by Flora Tristan. Her notes completed 1844, but not published until 1973. At her death, in the words of Jean Hawkes, she was mourned throughout France as the Workers' Saint. In this work she traveled around France, where she took the social pulse of the nation, addressed workers' meetings, and had interviews with clergy (we quoted her interview with the Bishop of Nimes in Chapter 2).

there is a fund-raising appeal using a song by Louis Festeau on page 205 citing in the refrain *Flora Tristan's Tomb*!!

Some links pertinent to Flora Tristan
A link to another photo of her tomb
http://es.paperblog.com/flora-tristan-en-recuerdo-de-una-masona-476854/

A link to a lot of her photos.
https://www.google.com/search?q=flora+tristan&biw=1366&bih=620&tbm=isch&tbo=u&source=univ&sa=X&ei=-XpmV OTSKda1oQTh9oDoDQ&ved=0CLMBEIke#facrc=_&img dii=_&imgrc=0o6iRcxWPA5aCLM%253A%3B3gqcEIprm9 5SrM%3Bhttp%253A%252F%252Fblogs.diariovasco.com% 252Fapartirdelos50%252Ffiles%252F313621_101503560943 52877_691382876_8562945_1956044187_n%255B1%255D. jpg%3Bhttp%253A%252F%252Fblogs.diariovasco.com%25 2Fapartirdelos50%252F2011%252F11%252F04%252Fcarn et_de_voyage_burdeos_3%252F%3B462%3B694

And there is a Place Flora Tristan between rue Sablier et Rue Bernard in the 14th Arrondissement de Paris, quartier Plaisance. http://fr.wikipedia.org/wiki/Place_Flora-Tristan

Another link to her place of interment, oriente eterno http://www.orienteeterno.org/2010/09/flora-tristan-en-recuerdo-de-una-masona.html

https://www.youtube.com/watch?v=d6qMaRB8haU
A promotional video for Sogamosa

http://www.colombia-sa.com/musica/musica-in.html
Mix of Colombian music

http://www.youtube.com/watch?v=I0o6b8501do
Bad roads that Emile may have built or re-engineered. Note
that the old, truss-style bridge could be of that era.

http://www.youtube.com/watch?v=TevKtD2AKh4
Road caused truck accident

En moto por Colombia: ¿donde carajos?
http://www.youtube.com/watch?v=htE0RXnMzMU
Stuck bus on mountain road

http://www.youtube.com/watch?v=Wjlapj8UvdM
Christmas celebration that looks like it is from former times.

http://www.facebook.com/video/video.php?v=1257946765523
Multi-stringed guitarlike instruments

http://www.youtube.com/watch?v=4m1VwxcOTpU
Marimba music in the Sogamoso zocalo with food vendors

https://www.youtube.com/watch?v=bupUHgJUD1g
history of Sogamoso railroads

pbs.org/wgbh/americanexperience/features/photo-gallery/
crash/ plus other video links to the 20's.

More online stuff:
El   Tiempo   (Bogota   daily   newspaper)   eltiempo.com/
seccion_archivo.

Jesuit-run thinktank CINEP.org.co

http://www.biography.com/people/simon-bolivar-24119

But what did EG miss in Denmark and Colombia during this time?

kulturarv.dk/1001fortaellinger/en_GB/theme/world-war-i-and-
the-interwar-period/article
en.wikipedia.org/wiki/1920s

en.wikipedia.org/wiki/History_of_Denmark
marketmonetarist.com/category/the-great-depression/in
Denmark

en.wikipedia.org/wiki/Roaring_Twenties   in   South   America
bing.com/images/search?q=roaring+twenties+in+south+amer
ica&qpvt=roaring+twenties+in+south+america&FORM=IG
RE images but nothing from South America.   Needs more research if the North American European sphere influenced the
Spanish/indio world of S. America.

Brinkley, Douglas. 2016. *Rightful Inheritance: Franklin D. Roosevelt and the land of America.* Harper Collins Publishers. New York.

Chasse, Charles. *1992. Gauguin sin leyendas, (Gauguin without Legends). No publisher or city of publication, no reviews could be found, but it is here to help another scholar. Note: the authors have seen this book referred to in a magazine article, we have not read it, and only learned of it in the magazine article.*

Dunkerly, James. 2000. A*mericana: The Americas in the World around 1850,* Verson, London. (Note: the book was recommended to us by Juan Nicolas Uribe because it refers to Bolivar, Paul Gauguin, and Flora Tristan. We have not read this book in its entirety, but have noted cogent passages on Paul and Flora.)

Dyrbye, Helen, Steven Harris, Thomas Golzen, 2008. *Xenophobe's Guide to the Danes.* Oval Books, London. (Note: this book was recommended by Michala Gauguin).

Earle, Rebecca. 2008. *The Return of the Native: Indians and Myth-Making in Spanish America 1810-1930.* Duke University Press, Durham.

Eisler, Benita. 2006. *Naked in the Marketplace: The Lives of George Sand.* Counterpoint, Berkeley.

Kaufmann, Hans and Rita Wildegans, 2008. *Van Gogh's Ohr: Paul Gauguin und der Pakt des Schweigens,* Osburg (Van Gogh's Ear: Paul Gauguin and the Pact of Silence). (Note: the authors have not read this book and cannot subscribe to its thesis which is discussed at length in the Art News link below. We chose to use this reference because it was the most recent we found on the topic. http://www.artnews.com/2009/09/01/what-they-see-in-van-goghs-ear/)

LaRosa, Chael J. and German R. Mijia, 2012. *Colombia: A concise Contemporary History.* Roman & Littlefield Publishers, Inc. New York.

Luke. Circa 100. In *The Gospel of Luke,* 22:49. In the New Oxford Annotated Bible: New Revised Standard Version with the Apocrypha. Oxford University Press, Oxford

Roca, Juan Manuel. 2000. *In Bogota: the ashes of Gauguin's sister.* http://ciudadviva.gov.co/portal/node/160 (Note: We found this is the article as reference 4 in Emile's Wikipedia article http://es.wikipedia.org/wiki/Emile_Gauguin) that allowed us to identify Marie Gauguin's grandchild, Consuelo Uribe, in Figure 2, to gain an idea about Maria Gauguin's first trip to Bogota and the hilarious rumor that Simon Bolivar was Paul Gauguin's grandfather. But we found a number of verifiable errors noted in the Appendix.)

Safford, Frank and Marcos Palacios, 2001. *Colombia: Fragmented Land, Divided Society.* Oxford University Press, Oxford.

Young Emile at 10 years of age (1884) according to his granddaughter
Mette Gauguin Fonseca who provided the Xerox of a portrait
taken in Copenhagen. A family picture of an older Emile with
his mother and siblings seen online show him to be wearing the
same style coat, likely the uniform coat of the Soro Academy.

Special Note: A Kindle version will soon be available
to aid readers to view and hear links as well as search
the text, and the photographs should be clearer.

Juan Nepomuceno Uribe Buenaventura, husband of Marie
Gauguin. The portrait was by the recognized French portraitist
Laurent. Born in Bogota in 1849, Juan died at the age of 47 in
1896 in Bogota. The portrait which now hangs in the home of
a family member was likely transported with other possessions
when Marie traveled from Paris. Photo was supplied by his great-
great-grandson, and engineer Cristian Perez Uribe-Holguin.

European Gauguin relatives with some of Emile's descendants
taken in 1987 at a family reunion in Copenhagen. Standing, far left
is Philippe Gauguin (Emile's grandson), standing, several people
to the right in the front row is Mette Fonseca Gauguin with the
white bracelet and gray coat (Emile's granddaughter), seated just
to the right is Aline (Emile's daughter), seated next to her is Pedro
Maria (Emile's son), standing directly behind is Mette Gauguin,
the painter from England (granddaughter of Pola, Emile's brother),
standing in the middle of the back row with a mustache and black
tie is Jan Gauguin (grandson of Pola, Emile's brother), standing
to the far left is Clovis with the beard (grandson of Jean, Emile's
brother), standing just to Clovis' left is his sister Maria with the
dark, shiny jacket. Photo provided by Mette Fonseca Gauguin.

Maria Elena Uribe, wife of Miguel Saturnino Uribe-Holguin
painted by the renowned portraitist Epifanio Garay of Bogota.
Emile who was living in Denmark at the time of her birth may
have known her if he visited his parents in Paris. The photo of
the actual painting hanging in one of the Uribe homes in Bogota
was provided by her descendant, Cristian Perez Uribe-Holguin.
We do not know the date of this painting, but the sad expression,
could be what the portraitist wanted, reflecting her emotional state
following the recent death (1904) of her daughter, Consuelo.

Emile and his son Borge Emile about two years in 1913 in Sogamoso.
Olga was pregnant with Pedro Maria when she snapped the
picture. It is possible Emile used this bridle and maybe the horse
in the Thousand Day War. A cavalry expert, Jay Eby (Prescott,
AZ), noted that the bridle is a European military type. The lower
set of reigns is to hold the horse's head down. The single strap
attached to the bridle just above the bit is a tether line used by
one trooper to secure a group of four horses taking them away
from the fighting while the other riders dismounted to engage in
battle. Photo was provided by grandson, Philippe Gauguin.

The wedding of Margot and Hernando Uribe-Holguin Uribe in 1945. Margot was the only Uribe we talked with who recalled a story about Emile when Maria Elena tried to have Emile marry her friend. She was born four years after Emile left Colombia. When we talked with her in 2014 at 93 she provided us with many genealogical details. Hernando was an officer in the army at the time of his wedding and later had the rank of captain while serving as an Aid to President Laureano Gomez. Later he became Consul to Monaco in Colombia. Photo provided by Juan Nicolas Uribe-Holguin Uribe. From l. to r.: Juan Uribe-Holguin Uribe, Elena Torres (mother of the bride), Maria Elena Uribe Gauguin (mother of the groom), the bride Margot, bride-groom Hernando (in uniform), and Pedro Uribe Gauguin (father of the bride).

Celebrating in their home Cristian Perez Uribe-Holguin Uribe
and wife Diana Perez Quijano proudly wear their team jerseys
after Colombia's 3-0 commanding win over a tough Greek
side in the 2014 World Cup. Off to a good start! Cristian,
an engineer and a great-great-great-great nephew of Paul
Gauguin, provided much help in assembling this book.

Travel document photos of Aline and Olga on the left and of
Borge Emile and Pedro Maria (l. to r.). Borge Emile was Mette
Fonseca's and Philippe's father. This document was dated 30 April
1918 in preparation for their 1918 trip to visit Emile in the US.
The boys in sailor suits had hats with actual ship names perhaps
to generate enthusiasm for the trip. No one looks happy, maybe
that was the style of document photos. But according to Emile
he was planning to have them emigrate which meant moving
to a strange place and giving up one's friends and family.

Emile at midlife in a series of poses most likely to
accompany job applications during the Great Depression.
He attached one of them to his 1938 letter to Maria Elena.
A Xerox was provide by his granddaughter, Mette Gauguin
Fonseca. In those times it was considered fashionable to
be holding a cigarette, and actually smoking it.

Left: Bitten Jensen Krentel and her good friend, co-author Frank's sister Kate in 1939 at the Malm's farm shortly after the Butterworth's moved to North Wales. Professional photographer, unknown).

Right: Co-author Frank in 1939 was four-years old, standing outside his 200-year-old house built with Pennsylvania fieldstone and hewn-log joists. He is looking toward the Malm's about a half mile to the right. Photo by Katie Butterworth.

Left: Priscilla and Emile at their wedding. This photo was typical of the time - weddings were serious occasions. Most likely the wedding was in the Philadelphia area, but no certificate is available, nor was it recorded in Katie's diary. No one we asked recalled the event.

Right: Emile and Priscilla all dressed up for dinner.

Left: Priscilla and Emile at the Butterworth's for Thanksgiving dinner in 1949. A year later they would move to Florida. Note the ever-present cigarette. Photo by co-author Frank.

Right: Frank in 1949 by the Butterworth tractor, a truck-tractor chimera that was completely renovated in a recent, multifamily project. Frank was 14 years old, in 9th grade. Photo by Frank's mother.

Pris and Emile relaxing on a hot afternoon. Emile, just got home from work, had removed his suit coat and tie. Pris is holding his fedora on her knees.

Left panel: Emile in the 1950's relaxing in his workshop with his sailboat under construction is just another example of Emile's handiwork. Photo taken by Priscilla.

Right panel: Emile sailing his boat. Photo by Priscilla. Both photos are part of the Katie Butterworth collection.

Pris and Emile by their 'Cookie' house in Englewood FL.
Near the end of his life he was dressed in fairly warm clothes
suggesting it was wintertime, but with flowering plants in the
background giving Florida the nickname of "Eternal Spring". The
photographer is unknown. Photo provided by Diana Harris.

Made in the USA
Columbia, SC
19 October 2023

24632130R00122